❦❧❦❧❦❶❦❧❦❧❦❧

PREVAILING PRAYERS OF INTERCESSION AND SUPPLICATION GUIDES

A Handbook Manual for Prayer Generals

❦❧❦❧❦❶❦❧❦❧❦❧

AKINBOWALE ISAAC ADEWUMI

Scripture quotations are taken from the HOLY BIBLE, KING JAMES VERSION (KJV)

ISBN 978-1-9994969-3-7

Editing and inner text design layout by Taiwo Adeodu +2348051106023

DEDICATION

"O that one might plead for a man with God, as a man pleadeth for his neighbour!" (Job 16:21).

To the Holy Spirit, the Commander-in-Chief
of God's Army.

TABLE OF CONTENTS

FAITH FOR FRUITFUL SERVICE
FAITHFULNESS FOR FRUITFUL SERVICE
DESIRING ETERNAL PRAISE

INTRODUCTION

INTERCESSION and supplication prayers are God's love in action and sacrificial too. It is the act of humbly pleading the cause of another or identifying with the travails of others so as to passionately present it before God in Heaven. Intercession, therefore, simply means the act of praying for others. This is one of life's highest and noblest callings and the greatest privilege ever offered to man such as was that of sharing Gethsemane with the Lord.

We live in a deceived world, a dangerous world, a defiled world and a divided world because of the activities of the devil as the god of this world. The devil, the archenemy of God and man, hinders men from salvation. Therefore, spiritual warfare which is an unseen and yet a real battle in the spiritual realm must be geared towards the rescue of the souls of men and women who are held in the captivity of satan. These captives comprise of various categories of people who are oppressed by satan and subjected to terrible afflictions and torments.

"Acquaint now thyself with him, and be at peace: thereby good shall come unto thee. Receive, I pray thee, the law from his mouth, and lay up his words in thine heart. If thou return to the Almighty, thou shalt be built up, thou shalt put away iniquity far from thy tabernacles. Then shalt thou lay up gold as dust, and the gold of Ophir as the stones of the brooks. Yea, the Almighty shall be thy defence,

and thou shalt have plenty of silver. For then shalt thou have thy delight in the Almighty, and shalt lift up thy face unto God. Thou shalt make thy prayer unto him, and he shall hear thee, and thou shalt pay thy vows. Thou shalt also decree a thing, and it shall be established unto thee: and the light shall shine upon thy ways. When men are cast down, then thou shalt say, There is lifting up; and he shall save the humble person. He shall deliver the island of the innocent: and it is delivered by the pureness of thine hands" (Job 22:21-30).

"How beautiful upon the mountains are the feet of him that bringeth good tidings, that publisheth peace; that bringeth good tidings of good, that publisheth salva-tion; that saith unto Zion, Thy God reigneth! Thy watchmen shall lift up the voice; with the voice together shall they sing: for they shall see eye to eye, when the Lord shall bring again Zion. Break forth into joy, sing together, ye waste places of Jerusalem: for the Lord hath comforted his people, he hath redeemed Jerusalem. The Lord hath made bare his holy arm in the eyes of all the nations; and all the ends of the earth shall see the salvation of our God" (Isaiah 52:7-10).

Spiritual warfare is essential to pull down the strongholds of satan and to release those kept within his strongholds. Believers in Christ Jesus have to rise and contend with this world on our knees and intercede for the

Church of God, leaders, saints, sinners and the nations for God's will to prevail over every situation. God expects every believer to intercede for others so as to turn judgement away from them and bring them to grace and peace with God. *"And I sought for a man among them, that should make up the hedge, and stand in the gap before me for the land, that I should not destroy it: but I found none"* (Ezekiel 22:30).

The passage does not mean man as a gender; it means the minister, pastor, Christian worker or anyone who has a relationship with God, either man or woman; male or female. It is known both in the Scriptures and in contemporary times that God uses women also as leaders in nation-building and intercessors. However, we must be in partnership with the Holy Spirit as He is the Spirit of love, intercession and supplication for others and ourselves. He is the indefatigable power behind the success of prayer ministry at all times.

CHAPTER

1

❧❧❧❧**❶**❧❧❧❧

REMOVING HINDRANCES OF THE WORKS OF THE FLESH

❧❧❧❧**❶**❧❧❧❧

"Now the works of the flesh are manifest, which are these; Adultery, fornication, uncleanness, lasciviousness, Idolatry, witch-craft, hatred, variance, emulations, wrath, strife, seditions, heresies, Envyings, murders, drunkenness, revellings, and such like: of the which I tell you before, as I have also told you in time past, that they which do such things shall not inherit the kingdom of God" (Galatians 5:19-21).

FLESH is one of the characteristic words of Paul which runs through his epistles especially those written to the Romans, the Galatians and the Corinthians. Its meaning, though varied, no doubt zeros in its being the most malignant enemy of the believer.

The works of the flesh are essentially associated with sin, evil and defilement. It, therefore, becomes obvious that to live in the flesh or produce works of the flesh is the precise opposite of being a Christian. The Lord, through Paul's epistles, taught the Romans then and us today: *"Ye are not in the flesh, but in the spirit...."* (Romans 5:9, 12). It is a contradiction to have a Christian producing and manifesting the works of the flesh. Now, what is the meaning of the flesh?

Meaning of the Flesh

"For we know that the law is spiritual: but I am carnal, sold under sin... For I know that in me (that is, in my flesh,) dwelleth no good thing: for to will is present with me; but how to perform that which is good I find not... I thank God through Jesus Christ our Lord. So then with the mind I myself serve the law of God; but with the flesh the law of sin... Because the carnal mind is enmity against God: for it is not subject to the law of God, neither indeed can be. So then they that are in the flesh cannot please God... For, brethren, ye have been called unto liberty; only use not liberty for an occasion to the flesh, but by love serve one another... This I say then, Walk in the Spirit, and ye shall not fulfil the lust of the flesh. For the flesh lusteth against the Spirit, and the Spirit against the flesh: and these are contrary the one to the other: so that ye cannot do the things that ye would... But chiefly them that walk after the flesh in the lust of uncleanness, and despise government. Presumptuous are

*they, selfwilled, they are not afraid to speak
evil of dignities"* (Romans 7:14, 18, 25; 8:7, 8;
Galatians 5:13, 16, 17; 2 Peter 2:10).

It is noteworthy and significant that the Bible speaks
of the works of the flesh. Work is something which a man
produces for himself. It is the opposite of fruit: a fruit is
something which is produced by a power which he does
not possess. The non-Christian, the backslider or the carnal
"Christian" lives in the flesh.

To live in the flesh is the exact opposite of living in
the spirit or being a Christian. More directly put, to live in
the flesh or produce the works of the flesh is to live under
sin, to be dominated by the flesh and to be *"sold under sin."*

> ❧❧❧❀⓪❀❧❧❧
> **The non-Christian, the backslider or the
> carnal "Christian" lives in the flesh.**
> ❧❧❧❀⓪❀❧❧❧

There is no hope from the sea unless one can obtain a
bridgehead. Temptation would be powerless to affect men
unless there was something already in them that responds
to temptation. Sin could gain no foothold in a man's mind,
heart, soul and life unless there was an enemy within the
gates who opens the way to the enemy who is pressing in
through the gate.

The flesh represents the whole system of corrupt
nature as it breaks forth into numerous forms of
transgression which are called the works of the flesh.

Works of the Flesh

"Now the works of the flesh are manifest which are these: Adultery, fornication, uncleanness, lasciviousness, idolatry, witchcraft, hatred, variance, emulations, wrath, strife, seditions, heresies, envyings, murders, drunkenness, revellings, and such like... Being filled with all unrighteousness, fornication, wickedness, covetousness, maliciousness; full of envy, murder, debate, deceit, malignity; whisperers, Backbiters, haters of God, despiteful, proud, boasters, inventors of evil things, disobedient to parents, Without understanding, covenantbreakers, without natural affection, implacable, unmerciful: Who knowing the judgement of God, that they which commit such things are worthy of death, not only do the same, but have pleasure in them that do them... For from within, out of the heart of men, proceed evil thoughts, adulteries, fornications, murders, thefts, covetousness, wickedness, deceit, lasciviousness, an evil eye, blasphemy, pride, foolishness: All these evil things come from within, and defile the man" (Galatians 5:19-21; Romans 1:29-32; Mark 7:21-23).

Of these works of the flesh, the first four - adultery, fornication, uncleanness and lasciviousness - come with greater force generally regarded as immorality. They are sins against the chastity of the believer, the entire body of

Christ and humanity. They are sins of sensual passion which the church has had to contend against in all ages and in all countries.

Besides, these immoral acts of fornication and adultery are among unnatural vices such as homosexuality, lesbianism, gay, bi-sexuality, trans-sexuality (LGBT) and other forms of perverted sexuality and uncleanness. These are also works of the flesh. Ceremonially, in the Old Testament, the unclean person cannot approach God. To seek to do this is to incur the wrath of God (Leviticus 22:3).

The lascivious person has lost all his sense of shame and decency. He openly, flagrantly and blatantly commits sin and defiles his body. He is indifferent to the voice of Scripture, unmindful of the voice of reason and insensitive to public moral opinion. A Christian found in lasciviousness has lost out to shame and he no longer cares what others say, see or think.

It is significant to note that it was with these sins of immorality that the list of the works of the flesh begins. Against sexual immorality, Paul's face was set and against this same immorality and uncleanness, the Church's face must be set today. It has been said that chastity was the one completely new virtue which Christianity introduced into the pagan world – (William Barclay).

❧❧❧❧❧ **0** ❧❧❧❧❧

The lascivious person is indifferent
to the voice of Scripture, unmindful
of the voice of reason and insensitive
to public moral opinion.

❧❧❧❧❧ **0** ❧❧❧❧❧

Our own church must also love to tell the world that a chaste life is the distinction of our membership. The church is called out of the world to live and preach the gospel of purity in a world in which the sins of immorality and perversion are rampant. In Paul's time, Christianity brought men into miraculous prayer to live in purity. We cannot have anything less than total purity in the church today.

Idolatry and witchcraft are works of the flesh that manifest themselves in illicit relationship with the unseen world. So, while the first four works of the flesh border on natural intercourse, the next two - idolatry and witchcraft – border on spiritual intercourse. It is significant that idol worship comes immediately after the group of words which describe the sexual sins.

In the ancient world, idol worship and sexual immorality were closely connected. Idol worship is the worship of created things rather than the Creator of all things (Romans 1:19-23). A man's God may rightly be said to be that to which he dedicates his time, his substance, his talents and even himself. Idolatry creeps into the believer whenever anything in the world begins to hold the principal place in his heart and mind: it could be a car, a certain brand of product, some ideas, the piece of furniture or some career.

The practice of witchcraft as a work of the flesh dates back to ancient times. It was repeatedly used by the Egyptian sorcerers and charmers who competed with Moses when Pharaoh would not let Israel go (Exodus 7:11, 22; 8:18). It was because of these works of the flesh – witchcraft, sorcery, and magic – that God foretold the destruction of Babylon (Isaiah 47:9, 12).

Christianity grew in an age in which the use of witchcraft and other magical arts were widespread. We read of magical experts at Ephesus in the Acts of Apostles (Acts 19:19): *"certain damsel possessed with the spirit of divination"* at Philippi; (Acts 16:16-18): *"a certain sorcerer, a false prophet, a Jew whose name was Barjesus"* at Paphos (Acts 13:6).

It was from this background that Paul declared that idolatry and witchcraft, wherever they are found – in the church or in the world, amongst Christian workers or amongst church laity; amongst the leaders in the church or amongst the members of the church - are works of the flesh and they must be extirpated. A living gospel Bible Church cannot accommodate witchcraft, either in the leadership or among the membership.

The next seven works or the flesh – hatred, variance, emulations, wrath, strife, sedition, heresies – constitute the sins described as breaches of charity. Hatred is the attitude of mind and heart which puts up the barriers and draws the sword between men within or outside the same church or community. It is the precise opposite of agape love – the supreme Christian virtue.

Variance and strife are the outward manifestation of hatred in the heart and mind (Romans 1:29-30; 1 Corinthians 3:3; 2 Corinthians 12:20). They are some of the works that are characteristic of the heathen lifestyle.

The world is a divided world, a world that is simply embittered at the sight of someone else possessing what he has not got. He would do his utmost, not to possess the thing, but to prevent the other person from possessing it.

Emulation is nothing less than ill-nature and embittered jealousy. It robs the believer of that blessed fruit of the Spirit called goodness. Wrath is the kind of temper that flares into violent words and deeds. It manifests in mad rage. It is the kind of uncontrollable human anger akin to those found in wild animals.

Seditions, divisions or dissension, as used in the churches of the New Testament, denote a state of relationship in which men are divided, feuds flourish and unity is destroyed. In the church, it is unfortunate to see seditions flourish. There is the personal division (among members of the church) and class division (among people of the same tribe, region or race amongst church members – 1 Corinthians 3:1-3).

It should well be that the greatest problem the church at present faces is the problem of her own disunity. This disunity is, however, certainly not only a problem but a sin - the Church's greatest sin. Furthermore, heresies are any personal practice or choice of belief or conduct which separates a man from the church which he is a part of. A fragmented Church is not a Church at all (1 Corinthians 11:17-19).

Drunkenness and revelling are Siamese twins of the flesh that always go together and which should not be mentioned among Christians (Isaiah 28:7; Ezekiel 23:33; 39:19). These vices normally accompany idolatrous practices of the heathen and they should not be so found amongst believers.

The works of the flesh are interminable. Added to the seventeen mentioned in our text are several "....*and such like"* (Galatians 5:21). The flesh is the breeding ground of all vices which man has or could ever conceive.

This explains why the list ended with "...and such like." The presence of the flesh in the man is a situation replete with several dangerous potentials. The church, as well as the individual believer who *"soweth to his flesh, shall of the flesh reap corruption"* (Galatians 6:8).

> The works of the flesh are interminable. The flesh is the breeding ground of all vices which man has or could ever conceive.

Breaking the Fallow Ground

> *"The night is far spent, the day is at hand: let us therefore cast off the works of darkness, and let us put on the armour of light... Sow to yourselves in righteousness, reap in mercy; break up your fallow ground: for it is time to seek the Lord, till he come and rain righteousness upon you... Therefore, brethren, we are debtors, not to the flesh, to live after the flesh. For if ye live after the flesh, ye shall die: but if ye through the Spirit do mortify the deeds of the body, ye shall live. For as many as are led by the Spirit of God, they are the sons of God...And all things are of God, who hath reconciled us to himself by Jesus Christ, and hath given to us the ministry of reconciliation"*

(Romans 13:12; Hosea 10:12; Romans 8:12-14; 2 Corinthians 5:18).

Fallow ground is an unused piece of land that accommodates different kind of weeds, thorns, garbage, pebbles, hard stones and strong trees with their stubborn roots. Many works need to be done before it can be used for agricultural practices. The land must be broken, cleared and tilled before sowing any crop or seed on it. This is what the unregenerate heart of man looks like; they are full of the works of the flesh which God the Father of spirits (Hebrews 12:9) cannot use until it's broken, washed and purged with the blood of Jesus. God cannot sow the works of the Spirit on the stony heart of man; it must be broken up before use. Stumps and thorns must be gathered together and burned. *"For thus saith the LORD to the men of Judah and Jerusalem, Break up your fallow ground, and sow not among thorns."* (Jeremiah 4:3).

The works of the flesh are offshoots of the sinful nature such as self-centeredness, subtlety, deceit, pride of life, hatred, sexual immorality, witchcraft, rebellion, wickedness, addictions and greed which are all thorns. They start with lust in the heart and end with outright, flagrant, shameless acts of lasciviousness. They are generally unnoticed or covert as hatred or envy but later come forth as outward works like strife or variance.

Saul started out with envy and ended up with murder and witchcraft. Whichever form the works of flesh might assume in our lives now, the necessary steps to take would be repentance, restitution and restoration (Ezekiel 33:10-12; Hosea 14:1, 2). The church cannot be clean if there is no confession, repentance and restitution neither will the Christian concerned be forgiven.

Fornication, adultery and uncleanness of all types are sins a man must repent of immediately or else his so-called Christian life and testimony becomes a mockery (2 Corinthians 12:21). The Christian must totally abstain from immorality (1 Thessalonians 4:3); He must shun it (1 Corinthians 6:18); He must put his evil deeds to death (Colossians 3:5). Sexual immorality is the one sin in which a man clearly sins against his own body (1 Corinthians 6:18) and the body is not for fornication. It is for the Lord (1 Corinthians 6:13).

In order to have the glory of God restored into our lives and churches, we must confess all the secret sinful lifestyle we have indulged and seek the face of God in righteousness for restoration into grace and fellowship. *"The Lord is nigh unto them that are of a broken heart; and saveth such as be of a contrite spirit"* (Psalms 34:18). A broken and contrite heart is what God desires from us. It is a true and living sacrifice of turning away from sin by totally forsaking and abandoning it. Such a person confesses all his sins and promises God never to return to it again. He carries his cross and follows Jesus Christ daily.

Therefore, unrepentant fornicators, adulterers or adulteresses, drunkards, liars, idolaters or the covetous who do not seek salvation, restoration or a return to holiness cannot be a prayer intercessor and shouldn't be a worker or leader in the fellowship of the children of God. (1 Corinthians 5:7-13).

It's high time for the Church as a whole to repent from lukewarmness, carnality and all works of the flesh that hinder revival. We need to seek the face of the Lord until He comes and rains righteousness upon His people. *"If my people, which are called by my name, shall humble themselves, and pray, and seek my face, and turn from their wicked ways; then will I hear from heaven, and will forgive their sin, and will heal their land"* (2 Chronicles 7:14).

Overcoming the Flesh for Spiritual Exploits

> *"For whatsoever is born of God overcometh the world: and this is the victory that overcometh the world, even our faith. Who is he that overcometh the world, but he that believeth that Jesus is the Son of God?... And be not drunk with wine, wherein is excess; but be filled with the Spirit... Seek the LORD and his strength, seek his face continually... And I will make an everlasting covenant with them, that I will not turn away from them, to do them good; but I will put my fear in their hearts, that they shall not depart from me"* (1 John 5:4-5; Ephesians 5:18; 1 Chronicles 16:11; Jeremiah 32:40).

The father-heart of God reaches out to every believer and every local Church to bring in a purge if the members repent of every work of the flesh in their midst and sincerely turn to God. Before we can live an overcoming life over every work of the flesh, we must first seek restoration (Joel 2:12-18; Amos 5:6, 15; Malachi 3:7).

Those who have turned themselves into agents of defilement in the Church luring members and ministers of the Church into the way of uncleanness, fornication, adultery, lasciviousness, hatred, variance and strife should turn to the Lord in repentance, consecrate themselves to holy living (Jeremiah 50:4, 5), remove all objects of sins and make restitution on whatever has been wrongly done, said or taken (Ezekiel 11:18-20; 14:13-20).

God is always delighted to see the church march forward militantly and triumphantly over every work of the flesh. The works of the flesh destroy the body of Christ which should be nourished and cherished. Members and ministers in the church owe the body of Christ a duty of living victoriously over the flesh. True holiness of life and the fullness of the Gospel light will be experienced and enjoyed if the whole Church can resolve to come into victorious Christian living.

Continual watching or eternal vigilance and prayerfulness are secrets of overcoming the works of the flesh. If we study the Bible and walk in the light as Christ is in the light, the blood of Christ will cleanse us from all defilements of the flesh and the spirit (1 John 1:7; 2 Corinthians 5:14; 6:1).

> Continual watching or eternal vigilance and prayerfulness are secrets of overcoming the works of the flesh.

Living an overcoming life over the flesh has two parts - there is the human responsibility (walking continuously in the light) and the sovereign grace (the blood of Jesus Christ His Son cleansing us continuously from all sin). *"Walk in the spirit and ye shall not fulfill the lust of the flesh"* (Galatians 5:16). The Christian walking in the Spirit will manifest the fruit of the Spirit – love, joy, peace, longsuffering, gentleness, goodness, faith, meekness, temperance (Galatians 5:22, 23). Bitterness and wrath, anger and clamour, slander and malice are to be put away (Ephesians 4:22). Anger, wrath, malice, slander and evil communication are some sins of the unbeliever and a Christian must have them eliminated from his life (Colossians 3:8).

Three lines of action then stand out for the believer who wants to continuously overcome the flesh. The first is deliverance from sin. God does this and we must experience it. The second is the denial of self. The believer must do this. It means saying, *"Not my will but Thine,* in everything connected with himself. The third is the discipline of sanctification. This is a process that involves both the believer and God working together. It's freedom from self (flesh) to love others sacrificially in service of God to humanity.

The believer grows in grace and holiness as he learns all through life what obedience to the will of God means even through pain and suffering of self-denial. The believer who wants to always overcome the flesh must simply remember that he is forever in the presence of Jesus Christ and forever seeks to make his life, action and decision fitting for Jesus Christ to see.

CHAPTER

2

৵৽৵৽৵৽0৵৽৵৽৵৽

PRAYER MINISTRY

৵৽৵৽৵৽0৵৽৵৽৵৽

"And in the morning, rising up a great while before day, he went out, and departed into a solitary place, and there prayed... And it came to pass in those days, that he went out into a mountain to pray, and continued all night in prayer to God. And when it was day, he called unto him his disciples: and of them he chose twelve, whom also he named apostles... Praying always with all prayer and supplication in the Spirit, and watching thereunto with all perseverance and supplication for all saints; And for me, that utterance may be given unto me, that I may open my mouth boldly, to make known the mystery of the gospel, For which I am an ambassador in bonds: that therein I may speak boldly, as I ought to speak... And in those days, when the number of the disciples was multiplied, there arose a murmuring of the Grecians against the Hebrews, because their

widows were neglected in the daily ministration. Then the twelve called the multitude of the disciples unto them, and said, It is not reason that we should leave the word of God, and serve tables. Wherefore, brethren, look ye out among you seven men of honest report, full of the Holy Ghost and wisdom, whom we may appoint over this business. But we will give ourselves continually to prayer, and to the ministry of the word" (Mark 1:35; Luke 6:12, 13; Ephesians 6:18-20; Acts 6:1-4).

PRAYER is an all-important ingredient in the life of every believer who not only wants to live victoriously above sin, satan and the world but also desires to be useful for God in building up men for Heaven. The saints of old were men who prayed and considered it a grievous sin if prayer is neglected. Samuel said, *"...as for me God forbid that I should sin against the Lord in ceasing to pray for you..."* (1 Samuel 12:23). No wonder they prevailed with God.

Prayer is the only way through which the soul of man can enter into fellowship and communion with the Source of life. Almost everybody sings "Prayer is the key" but very few can be with the Master "all night in prayer;" while some people, after hearing a message on prayer, will begin to pray but soon relapse into their former mental and mechanical prayer. There are Christians who know that prayer is the key to salvation, victorious Christian living, effective ministration, visions and passion for soul and of course key to "all things that pertain unto life and godliness," yet, they lack the zeal, courage and persistence in building up their most holy faith, praying in the Holy Ghost.

> ❧❧❧❧❧❀❧❧❧❧
> **There are Christians who know that prayer is the key to salvation, victorious Christian living, effective ministration, visions and passion for soul and of course key to "all things that pertain unto life and godliness," yet, they lack the zeal, courage and persistence in building up their most holy faith, praying in the Holy Ghost.**
> ❧❧❧❧❧❀❧❧❧❧

The ministry of prayer is opened to all believers. We learn to pray by praying. Begin at once and determine that you will continue to pray until a revival comes to your own heart. We shall consider three points in this regard.

Spirit of Supplication

"And I will pour upon the house of David, and upon the inhabitants of Jerusalem, the spirit of grace and of supplications: and they shall look upon me whom they have pierced, and they shall mourn for him, as one mourneth for his only son, and shall be in bitterness for him, as one that is in bitterness for his firstborn...Praying always with all prayer and supplication in the Spirit, and watching thereunto with all perseverance and supplication for all saints... Be careful for

nothing; but in everything by prayer and supplication with thanks-giving let your requests be made known unto God." (Zechariah 12:10; Ephesians 6:18; Philippians 4:6).

The word supplication comes from the Latin verb 'supplicare,' which means "to plead humbly" (https://www.vocabulary.com). It means to humbly submit our requests to God as Daniel did. The Spirit of all grace in believers inspires our prayers, reveals every need and stirs us up to pray in faith with fervency to have answers. The book of Daniel 9:17-18 and Romans 8:26-27 are instructive:

"Now therefore, O our God, hear the prayer of thy servant, and his supplications, and cause thy face to shine upon thy sanctuary that is desolate, for the Lord's sake. O my God, incline thine ear, and hear; open thine eyes, and behold our desolations, and the city which is called by thy name: for we do not present our supplications before thee for our righteousnesses, but for thy great mercies...Likewise the Spirit also helpeth our infirmities: for we know not what we should pray for as we ought: but the Spirit itself maketh intercession for us with groanings which cannot be uttered. And he that searcheth the hearts knoweth what is the mind of the Spirit, because he maketh intercession for the saints according to the will of God."

The Holy Spirit is the Spirit of grace and supplication Who awakens believers to their desire and their need to seek God's face in prayer. He is eternal, as the third person in the Godhead, He has all the attributes of God. He is Omnipotent, Omniscient, and omnipresent. He helps, intercedes for, comforts, guides, teaches, illuminates, inspires and gives us victory in temptation. No believer can do without the Holy Spirit and today, we can all receive the Spirit in baptismal measure if we:

- Thirst for it (Isaiah 44:3; John 7:37-38).
- Receive a new heart (Ezekiel 36:25-27).
- Exercise faith to receive (Mark 11:22-24).
- Pray to receive (Luke 11:13).

Paul the Apostle encouraged believers in Christ to take up the "full armour of God" (Ephesians 6:13-18); to remain alert and to pray in the Spirit unto God with faith because God is a Spirit and He wants us to direct all our personal prayer requests to Him. It is known as the prayer of petition while our prayer request on behalf of others is called supplication or intercession. It's also important to know that believers are implored to pray *"always with all prayer and supplication in the Spirit,"* the prayer that consists of confession, adoration, praise, worship, thanksgiving, petition, supplication or intercession.

> ৵৶৵৶❶৵৶৵৶
> Our personal prayer request is
> known as petition while our prayer
> request on behalf of others is called
> supplication or intercession.
> ৵৶৵৶❶৵৶৵৶

Praying Men

"Elias was a man subject to like passions as we are, and he prayed earnestly that it might not rain: and it rained not on the earth by the space of three years and six months. And he prayed again, and the heaven gave rain, and the earth brought forth her fruit... So also Christ glorified not himself to be made an high priest; but he that said unto him, Thou art my Son, today have I begotten thee. As he saith also in another place, Thou art a priest for ever after the order of Melchisedec. Who in the days of his flesh, when he had offered up prayers and supplications with strong crying and tears unto him that was able to save him from death, and was heard in that he feared... Moreover as for me, God forbid that I should sin against the Lord in ceasing to pray for you: but I will teach you the good and the right way ... Epaphras, who is one of you, a servant of Christ, saluteth you, always labouring fervently for you in prayers, that ye may stand perfect and complete in all the will of God" (James 5:17-18; Hebrews 5:5-7; 1 Samuel 12:23; Colossians 4:12).

In the Scriptures, examples abound of men who made indelible prints, changed circumstances, stopped the mouth of lions, received revelations and did exploits for their Lord.

God is still looking for such men and women in our communities, campuses, cities and countries today – men who would still the congregation of doubters, men who will persevere until there is 'sign of abundance of rain,' men of fervency and unwavering faith who will never let Him go until there is a blessing, men who will constantly fight spiritual battles against sin, against the desires of the flesh, against false doctrines and unscriptural practices in our society, against all oppositions of satan to the ministry committed to our hands.

Getting Involved Prayer Ministry

> *"And Jesus said unto them, Because of your unbelief: for verily I say unto you, If ye have faith as a grain of mustard seed, ye shall say unto this mountain, Remove hence to yonder place; and it shall remove; and nothing shall be impossible unto you. Howbeit this kind goeth not out but by prayer and fasting... And he spake a parable unto them to this end, that men ought always to pray, and not to faint... Continue in prayer, and watch in the same with thanksgiving... Be careful for nothing; but in everything by prayer and supplication with thanks-giving let your requests be made known unto God... Rejoicing in hope; patient in tribulation; continuing instant in prayer...Pray without ceasing"* (Matthew 17:20-21; Luke 18:1; Colossians 4:2; Philippians 4:6: Romans 12:12; 1 Thessalonians 5:17).

The challenging prayer life of our Lord Jesus Christ should be the model for every believer to follow. Like the disciples of old, we should humbly ask the Lord to teach us to pray. It is not enough to pray now. We must continue persistently in prayer until it becomes a habit, a duty and an expression of our relationship with God. If we are to maintain a prayer ministry, there must be great determination, discipline, self-denial and faith. (James 1:6; 1 Corinthians 9:29).

Watchfulness is necessary (Mark 14:38) we must always avoid sin because sin of any form will hinder us from attaining the height of our prayer ministry (Psalms 66:18). The spirit of jealousy or of unforgiveness, grudge, bitterness desire for retaliation will break the wings of faith and hush the cry of real prayer (Mark 11:24-26).

A callous conscience concerning some unpaid debt or an act of non-restitution has turned aside the incoming tide of blessing and grace from many a soul (Proverbs 28:9).

God will do nothing but in answer to prayer. Then prayer is the key. Prayer is everything. Let us pray (John Wesley).

God will do nothing but in answer to prayer. Then prayer is the key. Prayer is everything. Let us pray (John Wesley)

CHAPTER

3

꙳꙳꙳**0**꙳꙳꙳

DYNAMICS OF THE MINISTRY OF INTERCESSION

꙳꙳꙳**0**꙳꙳꙳

"I exhort therefore, that, first of all, supplications, prayers, intercessions, and giving of thanks, be made for all men; For kings, and for all that are in authority; that we may lead a quiet and peaceable life in all godliness and honesty. For this is good and acceptable in the sight of God our Saviour; Who will have all men to be saved, and to come unto the knowledge of the truth" (1 Timothy 2:1-4; Read Exodus 32:10-14; Jeremiah 2:18-22).

AN intercessory ministry is one of life's highest and noblest callings. It has been the weapon that mighty men of God used and are still using in averting God's judgement, changing the course of nature, turning men's heart to God and to righteousness and bringing God's blessings upon humanity.

It is obvious that great men of God in Bible days and years gone by who accomplished so much for God and their generation were men of a great burden for others. They were people easily moved by the needs and problems of others and never hesitated to carry all of these to God in prayer. However, it is alarming and unfortunate to observe that this ministry is fast becoming neglected or forgotten altogether.

> ❧❧❧❧ ❶ ❧❧❧❧
> **An intercessory ministry is one of life's highest and noblest callings.**
> ❧❧❧❧ ❶ ❧❧❧❧

The situation becomes worrisome because of the decaying spiritual state of this generation. Here, evil abounds in its sophistication and multitudes of souls are under Satan's oppression in our various environment. Today, myriads are rushing to hell daily. Laziness, indiscipline, selfishness, lack of compassion, absence of love and the cares of life have robbed many believers of the art and act of intercession.

God, more than ever before, is searching for men who will stand in the gap. He has made available all we need to engage in the intercessory ministry. These shall be considered in the following.

Meaning of Dynamic Praying

"So Ahab went up to eat and to drink. And Elijah went up to the top of Carmel; and he cast

himself down upon the earth, and put his face between his knees, And said to his servant, Go up now, look toward the sea. And he went up, and looked, and said, There is nothing. And he said, Go again seven times. And it came to pass at the seventh time, that he said, Behold, there ariseth a little cloud out of the sea, like a man's hand. And he said, Go up, say unto Ahab, Prepare thy chariot, and get thee down that the rain stop thee not" (1 Kings 18:42-44. Read James 5:17, 18; Acts 1:14; 6:4).

Dynamic praying is one that is effectual, fervent, consistent and result-oriented. It can also be described as a heartfelt, intense and agonizing praying that is directed towards the ultimate goal of receiving definite answers. It is a type of Christ's Gethsemane praying (Matthew 26:36-44); Abraham's intercessory prayer for sinful Sodom and Gomorrah (Genesis 18:17-33); Jacob's wrestling all-night in prayer for deliverance from his offended Esau (Genesis 32:9-30); and Hannah's outpouring of the burden of her soul for a man-child (1 Samuel 1:8-18).

It is a kind of praying that can change the course of nature as Joshua did (Joshua 10:12-14); a prayer that moves the mountain and knows no impossibility (Mark 11:22-24); a prayer that moves the hand of God. Contemporary saints have also left for us a monument of what dynamic praying ought to be.

Father Nash, Charles G. Finney, Madame Guyane, Katherine Booth, E. M. Bounds among others, have a challenging dynamic prayer life which transformed people, advanced the course of the gospel and positively affected the socio-economic life of their nations. Dynamic praying, therefore, can be summed up as giving oneself continually to prayer and persevering until the desired requests and petitions are granted.

> ❧❧❧❧❧**O**❧❧❧❧❧
> Father Nash, Charles G. Finney, Madame Guyane, Katherine Booth, E. M. Bounds among others, have a challenging dynamic prayer life which transformed people, advanced the course of the gospel and positively affected the socio-economic life of their nations.
> ❧❧❧❧❧**O**❧❧❧❧❧

Importance of Dynamic Praying

Dynamic praying is God's ordained means for extending His Kingdom *"And Jesus went about all the cities and villages, teaching in their synagogues, and preaching the gospel of the kingdom, and healing every sickness and every disease among the people"* (Matthew 9:35).

Dynamic praying equips us with weapons for defeating satan and his empire of darkness and evil and for fulfilling God's eternal plan and bringing His goodwill on earth into effect (2 Corinthians 10:3-7; Ephesians 6:12, 18; Matthew 6:6, 9, 10). It is also God's means of covering the earth with His blessing (2 Chronicle 7:14).

The history of the church can never be fully written until Christ, in eternity, reveals the mighty hidden prayer involvement of all His praying people - men and women of secret prayers (Matthew 6:6). Christ's current special divine vocation and strategic role is to intercede for us (Hebrews 7:25). The Holy Spirit also helps the intercessor become dynamic in his prayer life with groanings too deep for human expression (Romans 8:26).

Dynamic prayer is one of the most richly rewarding divine ministries one will ever be involved in. No form of Christian service is both so universally open to all and so high in God's priority for all Christians as dynamic prayer ministry. It is Christ's desire for, call and command to all Christians. (1 Chronicle 16:11; Isaiah 51:6; Matthew 7:7-1; Philippians 4:6; 1 Thessalonians 5:17)

Maintaining a Dynamic Prayer Life

"And Jacob was left alone; and there wrestled a man with him until the breaking of the day. And when he saw that he prevailed not against him, he touched the hollow of his thigh; and the hollow of Jacob's thigh was out of joint, as he wrestled with him. And he said, Let me go, for the day breaketh. And he said, I will not let thee go, except thou bless me. And he said unto him, What is thy name? And he said, Jacob. And he said, Thy name shall be called no more Jacob, but Israel: for as a prince hast thou power with God and with men, and hast prevailed... And it came to pass, that, when I was come again to Jerusalem, even while I prayed in the temple, I was in a trance... And it came to pass in those days, that he went out

into a mountain to pray, and continued all night in prayer to God... He took his brother by the heel in the womb, and by his strength he had power with God: Yea, he had power over the angel, and prevailed: he wept, and made supplication unto him: he found him in Bethel, and there he spake with us... Elias was a man subject to like passions as we are, and he prayed earnestly that it might not rain: and it rained not on the earth by the space of three years and six months. And he prayed again, and the heaven gave rain, and the earth brought forth her fruit" (Genesis 32:24-28; Acts 22:17; Luke 6:12; Hosea 12:3-4; James 5:17-18).

Prayer is the soul's desire for God (Psalms 42:1-2; 63:1-3), a cry, a supplication (Exodus 22:23; Psalms 34: 15, 17); an instinct that must have utterance (Isaiah 44:17-20; 45:20); an appeal from the child to the Father (Hosea 14:3; Matthew 6:6). It is described as beseeching the Lord (Exodus 32:11); calling on the Lord (Psalms 118:5; Acts 7:59); lifting up the heart (Lamentation 3:41): pouring out the heart (1 Samuel 1:15); seeking the face of the Lord (Psalms 27:8).

> ❧❧❧❧❧ ❶ ❧❧❧❧❧
> It is not enough to develop a deep prayer life; we must be able to maintain the same. Many started out, determined to be effective prayer warriors, only to lapse back into prayerlessness after some time.
> ❧❧❧❧❧ ❶ ❧❧❧❧❧

To be able to maintain such a life of prayer as described above is very desirable indeed. It is not enough to develop a deep prayer life; we must be able to maintain the same.

Many prospects started out, determined to be effective prayer warriors, only to lapse back into prayerlessness after some time. To maintain a dynamic prayer life, we shall consider the following.

The Importance of Maintaining a Dynamic Prayer Life

"Their heart cried unto the Lord, O wall of the daughter of Zion, let tears run down like a river day and night: give thyself no rest; let not the apple of thine eye cease. Arise, cry out in the night: in the beginning of the watches pour out thine heart like water before the face of the Lord: lift up thy hands toward him for the life of thy young children, that faint for hunger in the top of every street... And he spake a parable unto them to this end, that men ought always to pray, and not to faint... Pray without ceasing... And it came to pass in those days, that he went out into a mountain to pray, and continued all night in prayer to God... And from the days of John the Baptist until now the kingdom of heaven suffereth violence, and the violent take it by force. I have set watchmen upon thy walls, O Jerusalem, which shall never hold their peace day nor night: ye that make mention of the Lord, keep not silence, And give him no rest, till he establish, and till he make

Jerusalem a praise in the earth" (Lamentations 2:18-19; Luke 18:1; 1 Thessalonians 5:17; Luke 6:12; Matthew 11:12; Isaiah 62:6, 7).

The praying ministry is strengthened by continuity. A dynamic prayer life is one that is characterized by perseverance, importunity, persistence, faith, burden, compassion and zeal for God's work.

Anyone that desires to attain this result-oriented prayer life must have genuine and definite experience of salvation and other Christian experiences such as sanctification and Holy Ghost Baptism. Our sonship experience must be current (John 3:3, 5).

We must always maintain a clear conscience before God and man (Acts 23:1; 24:16). We should also be careful not to grieve the Holy Spirit who intercedes on our behalf (Ephesians 4:30, 31). We must be watchful so as not to relapse into bitterness and harshness of spirit; we must avoid engaging in unprofitable conversion (Ephesians 5:3-4).

Furthermore, every form of unhealthy criticisms of neighbours, colleagues, roommates, family members and others should be done away with. Another essential thereof is to check uncontrollable temperament such as clamour, loud-hard-rough speaking to mention a few. We must do away with every form of evil speaking, fault finding, tale bearing and the like.

To maintain a dynamic prayer life, we must avoid impatience, indolence, negligence and selfish personal ambitions that make the praying believer esteem worldly things more than heavenly things. (Colossians 3:1-2; Philippians 3:7, 9).

We must avoid self-dependence and self–management; rather there is a need to totally rely only on God. The praying believer must keep away from the sin of all sorts and all appearances of evil (Psalms 66:18; 1 Thessalonians 5:22).

More often than not, the praying believer must walk in the Spirit (Romans 8:6), be humble (James 4:6), be consistent (1 Thessalonians 5:17), study and meditate constantly on God's word (Matthew 4:4; Joshua 1:8; 2 Timothy 2:15).

Finally, there is a need to maintain inner holiness of life. Walking and dwelling with God in prayer call for a pure heart and clean life (Habakkuk 1:13; Psalms 24:3-6). We must also live a life of implicit obedience to God. There must be self-discipline and determination to pray always and persist in the same until the answer comes.

CHAPTER

4

❦❧❦❧ **0** ❦❧❦❧

DESCRIPTION OF INTERCESSION
❦❧❦❧ **0** ❦❧❦❧

"Praying always with all prayer and supplication in the Spirit, and watching thereunto with all perseverance and supplication for all saints... I will do these things unto thee, because thou hast gone a whoring after the heathen, and because thou art polluted with their idols... I exhort therefore, that, first of all, supplications, prayers, intercessions, and giving of thanks, be made for all men; For kings, and for all that are in authority; that we may lead a quiet and peaceable life in all godliness and honesty. For this is good and acceptable in the sight of God our Saviour; Who will have all men to be saved, and to come unto the knowledge of the truth" (Ephesians 6:18; Ezekiel 23:30; 1 Timothy 2:1-4).

TO intercede means to stand in between two people for the purpose of settling their disputes or to plead on someone's behalf in order to obtain something for the person being pleaded for. Intercessory prayer, therefore, simply means the art and act of praying for others and pleading to God on men's behalf.

This form of prayer makes us Christ-like because Jesus Christ devoted His life and ministry to interceding for mankind (Luke 23:34; John 17:1-26). At this level, the Christian is totally dead to self. He no longer desires that only his needs be met, but he persistently and consistently carries the problems, needs and burdens of others to God in prayer.

Intercessory prayer means crying with strong tears, moving the hand of God and standing in the gap for others. It is Abraham's kind of pleading for Sodom and Gomorrah (Genesis 18:17-33); Moses' falling flat before God for Israel (Exodus 32:10-14); Nehemiah's weeping and fasting for the state of the Jews and the broken walls of Jerusalem (Nehemiah 1:1-11); Daniel's prayers for the deliverance of the Jews in captivity (Daniel 9:1-23).

Also, it is Christ's apostolic prayer for the believer's sanctification (John 17:1-26) and His prayer at Calvary for the human race (Luke 23:34). It is a kind of Paul's prayer for the churches (Romans 1:8-12). These great intercessions were not men of doubtful characters or common Christian experiences. The qualities of their Christian lives and success in intercessory ministry are worthy of emulation.

Directives for Intercessors

"Love not the world, neither the things that are in the world. If any man love the world, the love of the Father is not in him. For all that is in the world, the lust of the flesh, and the lust of the eyes, and the pride of life, is not of the Father, but is of the world. And the world passeth away, and the lust thereof: but he that doeth the will of God abideth forever... Likewise the Spirit also helpeth our infirmities: for we know not what we should pray for as we ought: but the Spirit itself maketh intercession for us with groanings which cannot be uttered... I beseech you therefore, brethren, by the mercies of God, that ye present your bodies a living sacrifice, holy, acceptable unto God, which is your reasonable service. And be not conformed to this world: but be ye transformed by the renewing of your mind, that ye may prove what is that good, and acceptable, and perfect, will of God... Therefore I say unto you, What things soever ye desire, when ye pray, believe that ye receive them, and ye shall have them... But without faith it is impossible to please him: for he that cometh to God must believe that he is, and that he is a rewarder of them that diligently seek him" (1 John 2:15-17; Romans 8:26; 12:1-2; Mark 11:24; Hebrews 11:6).

The uniform testimony of the Bible and church history shows that great intercessors possessed some qualities that are necessary for dynamic intercessory ministry. There are some dynamics that must be present in the lives of every believer. These are some of the demands upon the intercessors:

i.   Sound and genuine Christian experiences. Ezekiel 36:25-27; John 3:3; 2 Timothy 2:19

ii.   Inner holiness of life (1 Thessalonians 4:7; Psalms 66:18; Luke 1:74-75) which will enhance boldness before God in prayer.

iii.   Strong compassion, passion and burden for others. (Romans 9:1-3; 10:1).

iv.   Unwavering, mountain-moving faith in the unchanging word of God. (James 1:6,11; Mark 11:23,24)

v.   Discipline, self-denial, ability to fast and pray (1 Corinthians 7:29-31)

vi.   Vision for the perishing, having in mind their eternal end (John 4:35; 1 Corinthians 9:16).

vii.   Desire to bring forth and contribute to the expansion of the Kingdom of God (John 15:16)

viii. Planned and regular prayer time. (Psalms 5:3; 55:17)

ix.   Willingness to identify and remove little foxes that eat up the appetite for prayer. (Songs of Solomon 2:15; Ephesians 4:31-32).

God's Search for Intercessors

> *"And I sought for a man among them, that should make up the hedge, and stand in the gap before me for the land, that I should not destroy it: but I found none. Therefore have I poured out*

*mine indignation upon them; I have consumed
them with the fire of my wrath: their own way
have I recompensed upon their heads, saith the
Lord God... And he saw that there was no man,
and wondered that there was no intercessor:
therefore his arm brought salvation unto him;
and his righteousness, it sustained him. For he
put on righteousness as a breastplate, and an
helmet of salvation upon his head; and he put
on the garments of vengeance for clothing, and
was clad with zeal as a cloak. According to
their deeds, accordingly he will repay, fury to
his adversaries, recompence to his enemies; to
the islands he will repay recompence... And
the Lord said, If I find in Sodom fifty righteous
within the city, then I will spare all the place
for their sakes... Run ye to and fro through the
streets of Jerusalem, and see now, and know,
and seek in the broad places thereof, if ye can
find a man, if there be any that executeth
judgement, that seeketh the truth; and I will
pardon it..."* (Ezekiel 22:30, 31; Isaiah 59:16-18;
Genesis 18:26; Jeremiah 5:1).

In every generation, God has always been searching
for men who could stand in the gap. He found an
intercessor in Abraham, Moses, Samuel, Nehemiah, Daniel,
our Lord Jesus Christ, Paul the Apostle and several others
that made marks in history. These Bible characters were
absolutely devoted to their intercessory prayer. Our Lord
Jesus Christ, Who is our model, was and is still the great

intercessor. His intercessory ministry for the Church continues even now that He is in heaven (Hebrews 9:24).

In our contemporary times, people like Father Nash, David Brainerd, John Knox, Andrew Murray, Susannah Wesley to mention but a few, virtually lived their lives on their knees pleading on behalf of others. They are men of like passion and we can be like them.

There are numerous blessings that await believers that will give themselves to the intercessory ministry. *"He that goeth forth and weepeth… shall doubtless come again with rejoicing, bringing his sheaves with him."* (Psalms 126:5, 6).

God is still searching for another Praying Hyde, John Knox, Father Nash, Susannah Wesley et al who will stand in the gap between God and the perishing souls in our countries. Who is on the Lord's side saying, "Give me this Land or I die?"

Prerequisites for Intercessors

> *"Though these three men, Noah, Daniel, and Job, were in it, they should deliver but their own souls by their righteous-ness, saith the Lord GOD"* (Ezekiel 14:14).

God is still searching for another Praying Hyde, John Knox, Father Nash, Susannah Wesley who will stand in the gap between God and the perishing souls in our countries. Who is on the Lord's side saying, "Give me this Land or I die?"

a.   Sound Christian experience. *"And he spake a parable unto them, Can the blind lead the blind? shall they not both fall into the ditch?... But as many as received him, to them gave he power to become the sons of God, even to them that believe on his name...For this is the will of God, even your sanctification, that ye should abstain from fornication"* (Luke 6:39; John 1:12; 1 Thessalonians 4:3; Read Joel 2:28).

b.   Vision for the perishing, having in mind their eternal end. *"Say not ye, There are yet four months, and then cometh harvest? behold, I say unto you, Lift up your eyes, and look on the fields; for they are white already to harvest"* (John 4:35).

c.   Passion and compassion for souls. *"I say the truth in Christ, I lie not, my conscience also bearing me witness in the Holy Ghost, That I have great heaviness and continual sorrow in my heart. For I could wish that myself were accursed from Christ for my brethren, my kinsmen according to the flesh...Brethren, my heart's desire and prayer to God for Israel is, that they might be saved"* (Romans 9:1-3; 10:1).

d.   Zeal for the work of God, knowing the shortness of time. *"I must work the works of him that sent me, while it is day: the night cometh, when no man can work"* (John 9:4).

e.   Desire to bring forth fruits and contribution for the work of the Kingdom of God. *"Ye have not chosen me, but I have chosen you, and ordained you, that ye should go and bring forth fruit, and that your fruit should remain:*

that whatsoever ye shall ask of the Father in my name, he may give it you" (John 15:16).

f.   Life of purity. "If I regard iniquity in my heart, the Lord will not hear me...That he would grant unto us, that we being delivered out of the hand of our enemies might serve him without fear, In holiness and righteousness before him, all the days of our life... For the grace of God that bringeth salvation hath appeared to all men, Teaching us that, denying ungodliness and worldly lusts, we should live soberly, righteously, and godly, in this present world;" (Psalms 66:18; Luke 1:74-75; Titus 2:11-12).

g.   Discipline and self-denial, ability to fast and pray. "But this I say, brethren, the time is short: it remaineth, that both they that have wives be as though they had none; And they that weep, as though they wept not; and they that rejoice, as though they rejoiced not; and they that buy, as though they possessed not; And they that use this world, as not abusing it: for the fashion of this world passeth away" (1 Corinthians 7:29-31).

h.   Planned regular prayer time. "My voice shalt thou hear in the morning, O LORD; in the morning will I direct my prayer unto thee, and will look up... Evening, and morning, and at noon, will I pray, and cry aloud: and he shall hear my voice" (Psalms 5:3; 55:17).

CHAPTER

5

❧❧❧❧❧ ❶ ❧❧❧❧❧

BURDENED HEARTS
AND BENDED KNEES
FOR THE PEOPLE
❧❧❧❧❧ ❶ ❧❧❧❧❧

"Their heart cried unto the Lord, O wall of the daughter of Zion, let tears run down like a river day and night: give thyself no rest; let not the apple of thine eye cease. Arise, cry out in the night: in the beginning of the watches pour out thine heart like water before the face of the Lord: lift up thy hands toward him for the life of thy young children, that faint for hunger in the top of every street... And he saw that there was no man, and wondered that there was no intercessor: therefore his arm brought salvation unto him; and his righteousness, it sustained him...And the Lord said, Simon, Simon, behold, Satan hath desired to have you, that he may sift you as wheat: But I have prayed for thee, that thy faith fail not: and

when thou art converted, strengthen thy brethren... Brethren, my heart's desire and prayer to God for Israel is, that they might be saved" (Lamentations 2:18-19; Isaiah 59:16; Luke 22:31-32; Romans 10:1).

A S the return of the Lord Jesus Christ draws closer day by day, the devil, not losing sight of the fact that time is short, has increased his strategies to keep perpetually in bondage individuals and families that are lost in trespasses and sins.

Many believers, including the leaders, have employed different methods of evangelism involving all the members in the local assembly with the view to rescuing the perishing. In the process, much energy has been dissipated in carrying out activities but with the little or no result.

An effective source of power for the deliverance of the lost to which many leaders and assemblies have paid lip service but tactically neglected is intercession. Believers who have the mind of Christ and seeing the multitudes of lost souls would be burdened in their hearts to pray with compassion to save them as Christ did.

> An effective source of power tor the deliverance of the lost to which many leaders and assemblies have paid lip service but tactically neglected is intercession.

In Matthew 9:36, "*...when he saw the multitudes, he was moved with compassion on them, because they fainted, and were scattered abroad, as sheep having no shepherd.*" If Church members and leaders will pay requisite attention to intercede for lost souls as Paul the Apostle was burdened about their condition, very shortly, the sinners shall be saved. A burdened heart would be full of compassion to bear the burden of others, most especially in prayers, as Christ did.

> *"Wherefore I also, after I heard of your faith in the Lord Jesus, and love unto all the saints, Cease not to give thanks for you, making mention of you in my prayers; That the God of our Lord Jesus Christ, the Father of glory, may give unto you the spirit of wisdom and revelation in the knowledge of him: The eyes of your understanding being enlightened; that ye may know what is the hope of his calling, and what the riches of the glory of his inheritance in the saints"* (Ephesians 1:15-18).

There are leaders in the Bible days that were burdened like Moses. In his earthly ministry, he interceded for disobedient Israelites until the anger of God was pacified. "*And Moses returned unto the LORD, and said, Oh, this people have sinned a great sin, and have made them gods of gold. Yet now, if thou wilt forgive their sin--; and if not, blot me, I pray thee, out of thy book which thou hast written*" (Exodus 32:31-32).

Satanic Oppositions

"And when they had gone through the isle unto Paphos, they found a certain sorcerer, a false prophet, a Jew, whose name was Bar-jesus: Which was with the deputy of the country, Sergius Paulus, a prudent man; who called for Barnabas and Saul, and desired to hear the word of God. But Elymas the sorcerer (for so is his name by interpretation) withstood them, seeking to turn away the deputy from the faith. Then Saul, (who also is called Paul,) filled with the Holy Ghost, set his eyes on him. And said, O full of all subtilty and all mischief, thou child of the devil, thou enemy of all righteousness, wilt thou not cease to pervert the right ways of the Lord? And now, behold, the hand of the Lord is upon thee, and thou shalt be blind, not seeing the sun for a season. And immediately there fell on him a mist and a darkness; and he went about seeking some to lead him by the hand... Wherefore we would have come unto you, even I Paul, once and again; but Satan hindered us" (Acts 13:6-11; 1 Thessalonians 2:18).

Satan energizes the ungodly to oppose God's will. He frequently attacks even the believers by weakening their zeal for evangelism, putting fears into their minds, discouraging them when the results of evangelism are not realized immediately. Old Testament experiences of Moses and Pharaoh clearly illustrates the opposition of satan.

The resistance and stubbornness of Pharaoh even after Moses and Aaron had performed many mighty signs and wonders also illustrated the extent the devil and his cohorts can go in keeping souls in captivity.

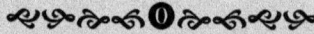

> ❧❧❧❧❧ **O** ❧❧❧❧❧
> Satan energizes the ungodly to oppose God's will. He frequently attacks even the believers by weakening their zeal for evangelism, putting fears into their minds, discouraging them when the results of evangelism are not realized immediately.
> ❧❧❧❧❧ **O** ❧❧❧❧❧

Instead of Pharaoh to release the children of Israel, he mobilized his magicians and sorcerers to oppose the power of God operating through Moses until they discover that "this is the finger of God" (Exodus 8:19). There are some organized powers and forces that militate against the penetration of the gospel of Christ in some areas.

"Finally, my brethren, be strong in the Lord, and in the power of his might. Put on the whole armour of God, that ye may be able to stand against the wiles of the devil. For we wrestle not against flesh and blood, but against principalities, against powers, against the rulers of the darkness of this world, against spiritual wickedness in high places" (Ephesians 6:10-12).

Some of these causes range from the spiritual to the man-made and the physical. These are: Satan's ministry (2 Corinthians 4:3-4); Saint's mistakes (Galatians 2:11-14); Location and origin (Acts 16:19-24); Organized persecution (Acts 4:18; 5:40); Dearth of selfless prayer (Ezekiel 22:30-31); Religion, social, political factors (Acts 21:27-32) and Activities of false preachers (Matthew 7:15). Satan always relishes his habit of keeping his captives in perpetual bondage (2 Timothy 2:26). He is the catalyst behind every resistance the missionaries encounter in the mission field as they strive to make sure that people are liberated from evil to fulfil the purpose of God.

This is why the Lord Jesus Christ confirmed that when an armed strong man keeps his palace, his goods are at peace. The devil is this strongman and souls of men are kept in bondage in his palace, using principalities, power, rulers of the darkness of this world and spiritual wickedness in high places. The disciples who followed the Lord Jesus soon realized that there are spiritual forces holding men in bondage as Philip encountered in Samaria where Simon the sorcerer held the whole city in captivity.

"But there was a certain man, called Simon, which beforetime in the same city used sorcery, and bewitched the people of Samaria, giving out that himself was some great one: To whom they all gave heed, from the least to the greatest, saying, This man is the great power of God. And to him they had regard, because that of long time he had bewitched them with sorceries" (Acts 8:9-11).

Elymas also opposed Paul in Paphos on his ministerial trip. Cults, agents of darkness and witchcraft activities are on the increase today, holding the souls of men under the yoke of the strong man. *"Now the Spirit speaketh expressly, that in the latter times some shall depart from the faith, giving heed to seducing spirits, and doctrines of devils; Speaking lies in hypocrisy; having their conscience seared with a hot iron; Forbidding to marry, and commanding to abstain from meats, which God hath created to be received with thanksgiving of them which believe and know the truth"* (1 Timothy 4:1-3). This is the end-time mobilization effort of the devil to gather souls into hell. Therefore, every soul-winner must be awakened to this realization in these last days and fight the battle for souls with passion.

Intercession in Spiritual Warfare

"(For the weapons of our warfare are not carnal, but mighty through God to the pulling down of strong holds;) Casting down imaginations, and every high thing that exalteth itself against the knowledge of God, and bringing into captivity every thought to the obedience of Christ... But if our gospel be hid, it is hid to them that are lost: In whom the god of this world hath blinded the minds of them which believe not, lest the light of the glorious gospel of Christ, who is the image of God, should shine unto them... Or else how can one enter into a strong man's house, and spoil his goods, except he first bind the strong man? and

then he will spoil his house" (2 Corinthians 10:4-5; 4:3-4; Matthew 12:29).

The devil is the strongman and the god of this world who took advantage of the fall of man to keep him in permanently in bondage. God has promised to do the impossible if we can stand in the gap. He will surely take the prey from the mighty because He desires to work hand-in-hand with His children.

> *"...stand in the gap before me for the land...Shall the prey be taken from the mighty, or the lawful captive delivered? But thus saith the LORD, Even the captives of the mighty shall be taken away, and the prey of the terrible shall be delivered: for I will contend with him that contendeth with thee, and I will save thy children. And I will feed them that oppress thee with their own flesh; and they shall be drunken with their own blood, as with sweet wine: and all flesh shall know that I the LORD am thy Saviour and thy Redeemer, the mighty One of Jacob"* (Ezekiel 22:30; Isaiah 49:24-26).

A burdened heart is compassionate and will always forget his own problem with a willingness to bear another person's burden. A burden-bearer is like our Lord Jesus Christ who groans and intercedes for others. God has made intercession a stirring summons to duty on the part of believers. *"I exhort therefore, that, first of all, supplications, prayers, intercessions, and giving of thanks, be made for all men"*

(1 Timothy 2:1). Intercession ushers in an overcoming force that dispossesses the powers of darkness of their captives.

> *"And when they had prayed, the place was shaken where they were assembled together; and they were all filled with the Holy Ghost, and they spake the word of God with boldness. And the multitude of them that believed were of one heart and of one soul: neither said any of them that ought of the things which he possessed was his own; but they had all things common. And with great power gave the apostles witness of the resurrection of the Lord Jesus: and great grace was upon them all"* (Acts 4:31-33).

Strategies for Interceding

> *"For which of you, intending to build a tower, sitteth not down first, and counteth the cost, whether he have sufficient to finish it?... Or what king, going to make war against another king, sitteth not down first, and consulteth whether he be able with ten thousand to meet him that cometh against him with twenty thousand?... Ask of me, and I shall give thee the heathen for thine inheritance, and the uttermost parts of the earth for thy possession"* (Luke 14:28, 31; Psalms 2:8).

When the Lord gave the Church the great commission, He knew the church will encounter some difficulties but he gave us the keys that unlock every door of a barrier to the preaching of the gospel. With the Saviour on our side and as we maintain a close relationship by allowing Him to lead us, victory is sure. Therefore, every battle to be fought requires planning and strategizing. Spiritual warfare is not an exception.

a. Identifying the lost – the religious, the idolaters, moralists or free thinkers, the worldly sinners and backsliders. *"Being filled with all unrighteous-ness, fornication, wickedness, covetousness, mali-ciousness; full of envy, murder, debate, deceit, malignity; whisperers, Backbiters, haters of God, despiteful, proud, boasters, inventors of evil things, disobedient to parents, Without understanding, covenantbreakers, without natural affection, implacable, unmerciful"* (Romans 1:28-31).

b. Figuring out the power militating against their salvation. *"For we wrestle not against flesh and blood, but against principalities, against powers, against the rulers of the darkness of this world, against spiritual wickedness in high places"* (Ephesians 6:12).

c. Pulling down the strongholds of such powers and taking authority over them. *"Thou shalt also decree a thing, and it shall be established unto thee: and the light shall shine upon thy ways…That at the name of Jesus every knee should bow, of things in heaven, and things in earth, and things under the earth; And that every tongue should confess that Jesus Christ is Lord, to the glory of God the Father"* (Job 22:28; Philippians 2:10).

d.   Pleading with God to open the eyes of sinners to the salvation which is in Christ Jesus only. *"In whom the god of this world hath blinded the minds of them which believe not, lest the light of the glorious gospel of Christ, who is the image of God, should shine unto them"* (2 Corinthians 4:4).

e.   Reminding God of His promises concerning the salvation of souls. *"Come now, and let us reason together, saith the LORD: though your sins be as scarlet, they shall be as white as snow; though they be red like crimson, they shall be as wool...For this is good and acceptable in the sight of God our Saviour; Who will have all men to be saved, and to come unto the knowledge of the truth"* (Isaiah 1:18; 1 Timothy 2:3-4).

Interceding for Nation(s) and Leaders

> *"Pray for the peace of Jerusalem: they shall prosper that love thee. Peace be within thy walls, and prosperity within thy palaces. For my brethren and companions' sakes, I will now say, Peace be within thee. Because of the house of the LORD our God I will seek thy good"* (Psalms 122:6-9).

This call was originally made to the inhabitants of Jerusalem but in reality, the Israelites were to pray for the city and entire nation of Israel. The word 'Jerusalem' holds a prominent place in the Bible and in Hebrew tongue; it means a city of peace. As God is a God of peace, it was a place they were expecting the Prince of Peace, the Messiah to establish His reign of universal peace, not only to the city but to the whole world.

As believers, we are called to pray for the peace of Jerusalem as well as the peace of every country we belong. *"And seek the peace of the city whither I have caused you to be carried away captives, and pray unto the LORD for it: for in the peace thereof shall ye have peace"* (Jeremiah 29:7).

In this verse of the Scripture, both nationals and foreigners are admonished to pray for the peace of the land they dwell. This is because there's no way we can enjoy our individual peace if there's violence in the city or in the land. Failure to intercede for the land may result in the country being overrun by violent people. Whenever there's violence or unrest, lives are lost and smooth services are truncated and the welfare of the people is disturbed. The reason God commanded us to *"Rebuke the company of spearmen, the multitude of the bulls, with the calves of the people, till every one submit himself with pieces of silver: scatter thou the people that delight in war"* (Psalms 68:30).

Our prayers will bring divine intervention for the God of Peace to reign in our land and bring peace, freedom from fear and terror; and spiritual prosperity for the individuals, families and the Church. The early church had rest because they prayed and there was peace and the Lord prospered them. *"Then had the churches rest throughout all Judaea and Galilee and Samaria, and were edified; and walking in the fear of the Lord, and in the comfort of the Holy Ghost, were multiplied"* (Acts 9:31).

Every believer in any nation has the responsibility to intercede for the land he lives in. He must seek the good and welfare of his country as this is the will of the Lord. *"Violence shall no more be heard in thy land, wasting nor destruction within thy borders; but thou shalt call thy walls Salvation, and thy gates Praise"* (Isaiah 60:18). Therefore, the challenge comes to us today and we must arise like Isaiah of old, *"For Zion's sake will I not hold my peace, and for Jerusalem's sake I will not rest, until the righteousness thereof go forth as brightness, and the salvation thereof as a lamp that burneth"* (Isaiah 62:1).

In the same vein, we are commanded to pray for our leaders and those in authority. This is because the throne of God Himself is established in righteousness and justice (Psalms 89:14) and He wants our leaders at all levels to understand the fear of the LORD and find the knowledge of God. *"I exhort therefore, that, first of all, supplications, prayers, intercessions, and giving of thanks, be made for all men; For kings, and for all that are in authority; that we may lead a quiet and peaceable life in all godliness and honesty. For this is good and acceptable in the sight of God our Saviour; Who will have all men to be saved, and to come unto the knowledge of the truth"* (1 Timothy 2:1-4).

The Scripture says, "first of all;" this implies, what is needed most and well pleasing unto God is to supplicate, pray and intercede for our leaders in authority. This is a command from God and not a suggestion. If we love ourselves and our land, if we want the best for ourselves and the people, if we really want them to be saved and want peace to rule and reign in our country, of first importance will be prayers of supplication on their behalf in the scale of preference and then the drive to ask God's fear and wisdom to work for them.

Successful Intercessory Warfare

"When a strong man armed keepeth his palace, his goods are in peace: But when a stronger than he shall come upon him, and overcome him, he taketh from him all his armour wherein he trusted, and divideth his spoils... Shall the prey be taken from the mighty, or the lawful captive delivered? But thus saith the LORD, *Even the captives of the mighty shall be taken away, and the prey of the terrible shall be delivered: for I will contend with him that contendeth with thee, and I will save thy children... And from the days of John the Baptist until now the kingdom of heaven suffereth violence, and the violent take it by force"* (Luke 11:21-22; Isaiah 49:24-25; Matthew 11:12).

The Lord Jesus has commissioned the Church to deliver the imprisoned souls through the guidance of Holy Spirit-led prayers. He has given the weapons to deploy and the assurance of victory. The Apostles tried this and came back with great testimonies.

"And the seventy returned again with joy, saying, Lord, even the devils are subject unto us through thy name. And he said unto them, I beheld Satan as lightning fall from heaven. Behold, I give unto you power to tread on serpents and scorpions, and over all the

power of the enemy: and nothing shall by any means hurt you" (Luke 10:17-19).

After Christ's ascension, the Church continued on the same pedestal and we, today, are bound to succeed if we all avail ourselves of all we are provided with in His word. Therefore, we can deliver the captives of satan, "The prey of the mighty can be delivered" and we can spoil the goods of the strongman with effectual intercessory prayers.

Bended knees in effective spiritual warfare will always produce a fruitful evangelistic ministry anywhere in the world. The gospel releases great power through those who are skilled in spiritual warfare; so also the believer who has faith in the name of Jesus and keeps the word of God will pull down every stronghold of satan. This is the secret of divine breakthrough.

> Bended knees in effective spiritual warfare will always produce a fruitful evangelistic ministry anywhere in the world.

As we engage in spiritual warfare, we would have a successful evangelistic ministry in every location, city and nation, even where satan's seat is. Sinners get saved, backsliders restored and the Kingdom of God expands astronomically.

CHAPTER

6

৵৽৵৹**0**৵৹৵৽

CONFRONTATIONAL PRAYERS

৵৽৵৹**0**৵৹৵৽

W E are in a battleground; that means war is going on all around us. It is an invisible war though. The effects are, however, visible - crises in individual lives, families, neighbourhoods, cities, villages, nations and globally. Even the church has not been spared.

The fall of spiritual giants, backsliding of once faithful saints, conflicts and splits in congregations, oppression, depression, and sickness among believers, spiritual poverty and lukewarmness and loss of evangelistic zeal are all results of the war the enemy has declared against the saints. This prayer implication of the satanic offensive is obvious: prayer must go beyond asking to seeking and knocking vehemently. However, these levels of prayers are unique and Spirit-directed.

"Ask, and it shall be given you; seek, and ye shall find; knock, and it shall be opened unto you: For every one that asketh receiveth; and he

that seeketh findeth; and to him that knocketh it shall be opened. Or what man is there of you, whom if his son ask bread, will he give him a stone? Or if he ask a fish, will he give him a serpent? If ye then, being evil, know how to give good gifts unto your children, how much more shall your Father which is in heaven give good things to them that ask him?...Let us therefore come boldly unto the throne of grace, that we may obtain mercy, and find grace to help in time of need...And in that day ye shall ask me nothing. Verily, verily, I say unto you, Whatsoever ye shall ask the Father in my name, he will give it you. Hitherto have ye asked nothing in my name: ask, and ye shall receive, that your joy may be full" (Matthew 7:7-11; Hebrews 4:16; John 16:23-24).

God is a good God Who always gives good things to His children. Why then are His children deficient of His abundance and sufficiency? The logical conclusion is that the devil lurks somewhere. He must be confronted. This then calls for knowledge, understanding and practice of levels of prayers that will make you dominate the dominator, oppress the oppressor, terrorize the terrorist and antagonize the antagonist successfully.

For too long, the church has been on the defensive; it is time for us to get on the offensive; to get into the enemy's stronghold, tear down his stronghold, bind the strongman and spoil his goods. Levels are used to denote the various forms of prayer that can be engaged in when interceding against the enemy.

> ❧❦❧❦❦ ❶ ❦❦❧❦❧
> This then calls for knowledge,
> understanding and practice of levels of
> prayers that will make you dominate
> the dominator, oppress the oppressor,
> terrorize the terrorist and antagonize
> the antagonist successfully.
> ❧❦❧❦❦ ❶ ❦❦❧❦❧

Confrontational prayers are those prayers that are directed against the enemy and his wars against us. You will learn about inspiration for confrontational prayer, issues for prayer confrontation, instances and ingredients of confrontational prayer. God desires to train you to become a prayer general, a terror to the devil and an overcomer. Someone has said that *"revival will come when we get the walls down between the church and the community."*

It is then time for you to learn about prayers that can be done outside the four walls of the church and the neighbourhood when you live school or work. God is taking into action praying. God wants to awaken the giant spirit that he has put on the inside of you. He will make you an end-time general in Jesus name.

> ❧❦❧❦❦ ❶ ❦❦❧❦❧
> For too long, the church has been on the
> defensive; it is time for us to get on the
> offensive; to get into the enemy's
> stronghold, tear down his stronghold,
> bind the strongman and spoil his goods.
> ❧❦❧❦❦ ❶ ❦❦❧❦❧

Inspiration for Confrontational Prayers

"For though we walk in the flesh, we do not war after the flesh... For we wrestle not against flesh and blood, but against principalities, against powers, against the rulers of the darkness of this world, against spiritual wickedness in high places... Submit yourselves therefore to God. Resist the devil, and he will flee from you... Be sober, be vigilant; because your adversary the devil, as a roaring lion, walketh about, seeking whom he may devour: Whom resist stedfast in the faith, knowing that the same afflictions are accomplished in your brethren that are in the world" (2 Corinthians 10:3, Ephesians 6:12, James 4:7, 1 Peter 5:8-9).

Our inspiration for engaging in prayer of confrontation is derived from the truth of the Scriptures; we are in battleground. We war against a formidable but defeated foe. The reasons for payer of confrontation, therefore, include the following:

1. To establish the Lordship and Kingship of Jesus (Revelation 17:14)
2. To counter satanic warfare (Romans 16:20)
3. To halt satanic encroachment on the Church (Ephesians 4:27)
4. To dispossess the enemy of souls for whom Jesus died (Matthew 12:29)

5.   To frustrate satanic agenda against believers, families, Churches and sinners (John 10:10)

6.   To break the operation of curses and oppression of many years (Galatians 3:13). Just as we had to appropriate the provisions of salvation into our lives in order to be saved, we need to apply that of sanctification to be sanctified. We also must claim God's promise of the Holy Ghost so as to get baptised and the free gift of divine healing in order to be healed. Moreover, it is necessary to appropriate the provision of deliverance from curses in order to break the unseen boundaries built around us to limit us. (2 Peter 1:3)

7.   To purge and purify the church (Deuteronomy 18:10-11, 22:18; 1 Peter 4:17)

8.   To heal the nations (Revelation 22:2)

9.   To protect our families and ourselves (1 Peter 1:5)

10.   To raise an end-time army of generals feared by the enemy and favoured by heaven (Ezekiel 37:10).

Instances of Confrontational Prayers

"By faith the walls of Jericho fell down, after they were compassed about seven days. By faith the harlot Rahab perished not with them that believed not, when she had received the spies with peace. And what shall I more say? for the time would fail me to tell of Gedeon, and of Barak, and of Samson, and of Jephthae; of David also, and Samuel, and of the prophets: Who through faith subdued king-doms, wrought righteousness, obtained

promises, stopped the mouths of lions. Quenched the violence of fire, escaped the edge of the sword, out of weakness were made strong, waxed valiant in fight, turned to flight the armies of the aliens" (Hebrews 11:30-34).

Instances abound in the Scriptures where the apostles, prophets and the Lord Jesus engaged in confrontational prayer.

Jesus Christ in the garden and on the cross engaged in prayer of confrontation (Colossians 2:14-15; Luke 22:41-44; 19:27).

Apostle Paul fought with beasts in Ephesus and made Elymas the sorcerer blind for a season or a year in Paphos.

"...If after the manner of men I have fought with beasts at Ephesus, what advantageth it me, if the dead rise not? let us eat and drink; for to morrow we die... (1 Corinthians 15:32).

6 And when they had gone through the isle unto Paphos, they found a certain sorcerer, a false prophet, a Jew, whose name was Barjesus:

7 Which was with the deputy of the country, Sergius Paulus, a prudent man; who called for Barnabas and Saul, and desired to hear the word of God.

8 But Elymas the sorcerer (for so is his name by interpretation) withstood them, seeking to turn away the deputy from the faith.

9 Then Saul, (who also is called Paul,) filled with the Holy Ghost, set his eyes on him,

10 And said, O full of all subtilty and all mischief, thou child of the devil, thou enemy of all righteousness, wilt thou not cease to pervert the right ways of the Lord?

11 And now, behold, the hand of the Lord is upon thee, and thou shalt be blind, not seeing the sun for a season. And immediately there fell on him a mist and a darkness; and he went about seeking some to lead him by the hand.

12 Then the deputy, when he saw what was done, believed, being astonished at the doctrine of the Lord" (Acts 13:6-12).

"Alexander the coppersmith did me much evil: the Lord reward him according to his works:" (2 Timothy 4:14).

Apostle Peter pronounced a death sentence on a lying couple – Ananias and Sapphira, in the early Church.

"1 But a certain man named Ananias, with Sapphira his wife, sold a possession,

2 And kept back part of the price, his wife also being privy to it, and brought a certain part, and laid it at the apostles' feet.

3 But Peter said, Ananias, why hath Satan filled thine heart to lie to the Holy Ghost, and to keep back part of the price of the land?

4 Whiles it remained, was it not thine own? and after it was sold, was it not in thine own power? why hast thou conceived this thing in thine heart? thou hast not lied unto men, but unto God.

5 And Ananias hearing these words fell down, and gave up the ghost: and great fear came on all them that heard these things.

6 And the young men arose, wound him up, and carried him out, and buried him.

7 And it was about the space of three hours after, when his wife, not knowing what was done, came in.

8 And Peter answered unto her, Tell me whether ye sold the land for so much? And she said, Yea, for so much.

9 Then Peter said unto her, How is it that ye have agreed together to tempt the Spirit of the Lord? behold, the feet of them which have buried thy husband are at the door, and shall carry thee out.

10 Then fell she down straightway at his feet, and yielded up the ghost: and the young men came in, and found her dead, and, carrying her forth, buried her by her husband.

11 And great fear came upon all the church, and upon as many as heard these things.

12 And by the hands of the apostles were many signs and wonders wrought among the people; (and they were all with one accord in Solomon's porch" (Acts 5:1-12).

> ❧❧❧❧❧ ⓪ ❧❧❧❧❧
> Apostle Paul made Elymas the sorcerer
> blind for a season or a year in Paphos.
> Apostle Peter pronounced a death
> sentence on a lying couple – Ananias and
> Sapphira, in the early Church. The
> Church prayed a dangerous prayer of
> confrontation and God sent an angel to
> kill Herod the king after he had executed
> James the brother of John and also
> imprisoned Peter.
> ❧❧❧❧❧ ⓪ ❧❧❧❧❧

The Church prayed a dangerous prayer of confrontation and God sent an angel to kill Herod the king after he had executed James the brother of John and also imprisoned Peter.

"1 Now about that time Herod the king stretched forth his hands to vex certain of the church.

2 And he killed James the brother of John with the sword.

3 And because he saw it pleased the Jews, he proceeded further to take Peter also. (Then were the days of unleavened bread.)

20 And Herod was highly displeased with them of Tyre and Sidon: but they came with one accord to him, and, having made Blastus the king's chamberlain their friend, desired peace;

because their country was nourished by the king's country.

21 And upon a set day Herod, arrayed in royal apparel, sat upon his throne, and made an oration unto them.

22 And the people gave a shout, saying, It is the voice of a god, and not of a man.

23 And immediately the angel of the Lord smote him, because he gave not God the glory: and he was eaten of worms, and gave up the ghost.

24 But the word of God grew and multiplied" (Acts 12:1-3, 20-24).

David defended the name of God when he confronted the Philistine general and Elijah confronted Ahab, Jezebel, Baal's prophets, Ahaziah (1 Kings 17:1, 18:8, 16-24, 30-34; 2 Kings 1:1-17).

Elisha confronted the Jordanian barrier (2 Kings 2:13-14).

Joshua confronted elemental and extra-galactic powers (Joshua 10:12-13).

The apostles confronted opposition. These are our examples. The New Testament is replete with instances where believers engaged in spiritual warfare (2 Corinthians 10:3). They wrestle (Ephesians 6:12) and stood their ground as true soldiers at their posts (2 Timothy 2:2); and always remained overcomers of the devil and his cohorts (Revelations 12:11).

Issues for Prayers of Confrontation

"And from the days of John the Baptist until now the kingdom of heaven suffereth violence, and the violent take it by force. "(Matthew 12:11).

There are issues in life and ministry that do not demand a gentle approach of the "sweet hour of prayer." We should make prayer confrontational when:

1. The name and glory of Jehovah is challenged (Daniel 3:15-18)
2. You want to take the Kingdom of God (Matthew 11:12)
3. You sense satanic resistance (Zechariah 3:1-2)
4. Life is in danger (Psalms 106:9; Mark 4:39)
5. There are satanic strongholds and encampment to be demolished or dislodged (Jeremiah 51:20-26; 30:16-17)
6. You desire righteousness over rottenness and revival over religious formalism (Colossians 1:10; Philippians 3:9)
7. You want to move up in your walk with God and in the height of God's maximum for your life (Philippians 3:11-14)

Ingredients for Effective Prayers of Confrontation

"And the things that thou hast heard of me among many witnesses, the same commit thou to faithful men, who shall be able to teach others also. Thou therefore endure hardness, as

a good soldier of Jesus Christ. No man that warreth entangleth himself with the affairs of this life; that he may please him who hath chosen him to be a soldier. And if a man also strive for masteries, yet is he not crowned, except he strive lawfully...If a man therefore purge himself from these, he shall be a vessel unto honour, sanctified, and meet for the master's use, and prepared unto every good work" (2 Timothy 2:2-5, 21).

Confrontational prayer is not effective by power or by might; or by assumption, presumption or putting up a bold front. Essentially, effective prayer confrontation is achieved through:

1. Repentance and obedience - Acts 19:18-20; 2 Corinthians 10:6

2. Righteousness and holiness - Ephesians. 6:14

3. Faith - 1 Peter 5:8-9

4. Fasting - Matthew 17:21

5. Divine unity - Psalms 133:1; Matthew 18:19

6. Prophetic utterance, urgings, inspiration and ministry - 2 Chronicles 20:14-17

7. Praise - Psalms 144:9-10

8. Divine legislation – Psalms 1119:34-35

9. Delegated authority - Luke 9:1; 10:19

10. High tension anointing – 1 Kings 18:38

11. The sword of the Spirit - Ephesians 6:17

12. By the blood of the lamb - Revelation 12:11

CHAPTER

7

꿍ᢌᢌᢌ**0**ᢌᢌᢌ꿍

PRAYING LIKE GOD'S END-TIME GENERALS

꿍ᢌᢌᢌ**0**ᢌᢌᢌ꿍

IN James 5:16-17, the Bible says, "*Confess your faults one to another, and pray one for another, that ye may be healed. The effectual fervent prayer of a righteous man availeth much. Elias was a man subject to like passions as we are, and he prayed earnestly that it might not rain: and it rained not on the earth by the space of three years and six months.*"

Jesus Christ died to make sheep for the Great Shepherd. As sheep, we are meek but not weaklings to be plundered by the roaring lion at will. The believers are chosen to be prayer soldiers.

The body of Christ in the end-time will manifest as battering rams of spiritual generals. Christ did not die to raise up believers defiled by sin, deformed by sickness and destroyed by satan. He died to raise up an exceedingly great army (Ezekiel 37:10). You are God's end-time general.

The devil may have his principalities and power but we are God's princes (princesses) and power house. The devil should not dictate the pace of events; the believers should call the shots. The time has come for us to outmatch the enemy fire for fire, and bullet for bullet. We are the generals who will change the world. To do that, you must learn how to pray confrontationally as God's end-time generals.

> ❧❧❧❧❧**O**❧❧❧❧❧
> **Christ did not die to raise up believers defiled by sin, deformed by sickness and destroyed by satan. He died to raise up an exceedingly great army.**
> ❧❧❧❧❧**O**❧❧❧❧❧

Lessons from a Prayer General

There are seven key lessons to learn from the three verses of James 5:16-18;

"Confess your faults one to another, and pray one for another, that ye may be healed. The effectual fervent prayer of a righteous man availeth much. Elias was a man subject to like passions as we are, and he prayed earnestly that it might not rain: and it rained not on the earth by the space of three years and six months. And he prayed again, and the heaven gave rain, and the earth brought forth her fruit."

In these three short but inspiring verses, the Holy Spirit reflects on the prayer ministry of Elijah, who was

God's general in his generation. He appeared from obscurity and issued a decree. *As the Lord God of Israel liveth before whom I stand, there shall not be dew nor rain these years but according to my word.* Elijah locked and unlocked heaven. He prayed and fire fell, kings fell, queens fell, false prophets fell and Israel fell with a confession that *"The Lord he is the God."* The Lord, He is God. Let's be guided that:

> ❧❧❀❀❖❀❀❧❧
> The time has come for us to outmatch the enemy fire for fire, and bullet for bullet. We are the generals who will change the world. To do that, you must learn how to pray confrontationally as God's end-time generals.
> ❧❧❀❀❖❀❀❧❧

1. God's generals are ordinary people: James 5:17. *"Elias was a man subject to like passions as we are."* David was a man. Samson, Adina, Eleazar, Shammah, Abishai and Benaiah were all God's generals in their time. Deborah, Kathryn Kuhlman and Aimee Semple McPherson were mightily used of God. They carried incredible voltage of God's power to heal and deliver. When Linda Prince prayed, the sky split and the devil shuddered. Praying Hyde prayed souls into the Kingdom on a daily basis. If they did, you can; if God used them, He also can use you.

2. God's generals are people of earnest prayer: James 5:17 Elias – *"...he prayed earnestly"* - This means that in

praying, he prayed. He was involved in his praying. He prayed with a determination to win. Prayer was a serious business that demanded absolute concentration. We must be involved in our praying and cooperate with our prayers if we would do exploits. We must pray to win and concentrate 100% while praying within or without.

3. God's generals pray purposefully and in a revolutionary way: James 5:17, Elias… prayed that it might not rain. He was specific. No rain. He was revolutionary because a nation that refused to worship the God of Heaven should not receive the blessing of Heaven. The lesson here is that power will fall where payer is focussed.

4. God's generals pray consistently: James 5:18. *"And he prayed again."* It was at the seventh time of prayer that the rains came. He prayed consistently and with consecration. Power and blessing will fall if God's end-time generals will learn the secret of importunate praying.

5. God's general's prayer has fire-power: James 16b. *"the effectual fervent prayer"* - They prayed in spirit with passion. Effectual is translated from the Greek word 'energo' meaning divine energy. Elijah's prayer was too hot for the devil to handle.

6. God's generals are righteous people: *"...The effectual fervent prayer of a righteous man availeth much"* (James 5:16b).

    In the effectual fervent prayer of a righteous man - righteousness was their strength. It must be ours also. We cannot be strong prayer generals if holiness is not in our hearts and righteousness in our lives. *"The righteous also shall hold on his way, and he that hath clean hands shall be stronger and stronger... The wicked flee when no man pursueth: but the righteous are bold as a lion... That he would grant unto us, that we being delivered out of the hand of our enemies might serve him without fear, In holiness and righteousness before him, all the days of our life"* (Job 17:9; Proverbs 28:1; Luke 1:74-75).

7. God's generals' prayer accomplishes great results. James 5:16 says, *"The effectual fervent prayer of a righteous man availeth much."* Another translation says the prayer of a righteous has a powerful effect if one prays as God's generals do.

Becoming God's End-time General

> *"Take my yoke upon you, and learn of me; for I am meek and lowly in heart: and ye shall find rest unto your souls... And it came to pass, that, as he was praying in a certain place, when he ceased, one of his disciples said unto him, Lord, teach us to pray, as John also taught his disciples. And he said unto them, When ye pray, say, Our Father which art in heaven, Hallowed be thy name. Thy kingdom come. Thy will be*

done, as in heaven, so in earth" (Matthew 11:29;
Luke 11:1-2; Read also 2 Samuel 23:8-23; Psalms
18:29-50).

No soldier ever becomes a general the day he enlists
in the military. A general is a military commander who has
accumulated knowledge and experience in the principles
and practices of warfare. The disciples requested, "Lord
teach us to pray" while the Lord commanded in another
place, "Learn of me."

The following steps and lifestyle are essential for
those who are determined to count in God's end-time army.

1. **Enlistment**: In 2 Timothy 2:2, *"And the things that thou
hast heard of me among many witnesses, the same commit thou to
faithful men, who shall be able to teach others also."*

2. **Reconnaissance**: Recognizes there is an enemy. This
enemy is called (a) the accuser (b) an adversary (c) the angel
of the bottomless pit (d) Apollyon (e) Abaddon
(f) Beelzebeb (g) Belial (h) an evil spirit (i) a murderer
and thief. He is also considered as (j) a fowler (k) a bird of
the air (l) the god of this world (m) a roaring lion (n) the old
serpent (o) the dragon and (p) the deceiver. This is the real
enemy we confront in prayer. Recognize your enemies'
strategy - 2 Corinthians 2:11.

3. **Reveille**: This is the music or sound signal that wakes
up the soldier to his daily duties. We must begin each day
with prayer. Psalms 5:3; Joel 2:15-17; 3:9-12

4.   **Fasting and seasons of prayer:** Strategic fasting and prayer are spiritual exercises that strengthen the spiritual muscles of disciplined soldiers of the cross. We must be consistent in prayer though without tiring out. Matthew 17:21; 1 Thessalonians 5:17; Colossians 4:2; Luke 18:1; Romans 12:12

> ❧❧❧❧**O**❧❧❧❧
> No soldier ever becomes a general the day he enlists in the military. A general is a military commander who has accumulated knowledge and experience in the principles and practices of warfare.
> ❧❧❧❧**O**❧❧❧❧

5.   **Territorial dominion:** Soldiers are meant to protect and defend the territorial integrity of their country. Generals, as experts in warfare, know that this is all too important for the safety of life and property of citizens. Ephesians 4:27

6.   **Right attitude:** Attitude, they say, is everything and the right one for that matter. It could be summarized as a tactical combination of character and charisma as listed below. 2 Timothy 2:2-7

➤   obedience - 1 Samuel 15:22
➤   submission - James 4:7
➤   faithfulness - 2 Corinthians 4:2; 2 Timothy 2:2

➢ holiness - Leviticus 20:7; 1 Peter 1:15-16
➢ integrity - John 14:30
➢ communication - Hebrews 10:25
➢ ruggedness - 2 Timothy 2:3
➢ commitment to win - 2 Samuel 23:10,
➢ consecration - 2 Timothy 2:4
➢ forgiveness - Mark 11:25
➢ boldness - Proverbs 28:1b; Hebrews 4:16; 2 Samuel 23:20-23

7.   **Anointing for the battle of the end-time**: The anointing is the quickening Spirit and the Divine blood that flows in the believer's veins. The Word of God is the Constitution while the Anointing is Consitutionalism – the Spirit of the Constitution. The Christian heart is God's altar and the Holy Ghost is the living flame burning on it. John 6:63; 1 John 2:20, 27

CHAPTER

8

❧❧❧❧ **0** ❧❧❧❧

PRAYER WATCHES

❧❧❧❧ **0** ❧❧❧❧

"I will stand upon my watch, and set me upon the tower, and will watch to see what he will say unto me, and what I shall answer when I am reproved. And the LORD answered me, and said, Write the vision, and make it plain upon tables, that he may run that readeth it. For the vision is yet for an appointed time, but at the end it shall speak, and not lie: though it tarry, wait for it; because it will surely come, it will not tarry... I have set watchmen upon thy walls, O Jerusalem, which shall never hold their peace day nor night: ye that make mention of the LORD, keep not silence, And give him no rest, till he establish, and till he make Jerusalem a praise in the earth...Also I set watchmen over you, saying, Hearken to the sound of the trumpet. But they said, We will not hearken... Son of man, I have made thee a watchman unto the house of Israel: therefore hear the word at my mouth, and give them

warning from me... And in the morning, rising up a great while before day, he went out, and departed into a solitary place, and there prayed" (Habakkuk 2:1-3; Isaiah 62:6-7; Jeremiah 6:17; Ezekiel 3:17, Mark 1:35; Read also Mark 6:46; Luke 6:12-16; 11:11; Matthew 14:23-25).

A PRAYER watch is a specific period which a believer sets apart for the purpose of prayer, waiting upon God and fellowship with God on certain issues pertaining to life, family, ministry, vision and key decisions. It could be in the day or night but the night season is always more effective because of less distraction and more concentration. For those who have a calling to the ministry of intercession, prayer watch is a God-appointed responsibility and obligation (Isaiah 62:6-7).

If we are sensitive to the leading and revelation of the Holy Spirit and acknowledge our entire dependence on God for guidance and empowerment, we would, no doubt, learn, love and practice prayer watches. If Jesus Christ did, we must (Luke 6:12-16, 1 Peter 2:21). However, to profit maximally from payer watches, we have to understand the purpose, practice and principle of effective prayer watches.

Purpose of Prayer Watches

"I will stand upon my watch, and set me upon the tower, and will watch to see what he will say unto me, and what I shall answer when I am reproved. And the LORD answered me, and said, Write the vision, and make it plain upon

tables, that he may run that readeth it. For the vision is yet for an appointed time, but at the end it shall speak, and not lie: though it tarry, wait for it; because it will surely come, it will not tarry... And when it was day, he called unto him his disciples: and of them he chose twelve, whom also he named apostles... And give him no rest, till he establish, and till he make Jerusalem a praise in the earth... For Zion's sake will I not hold my peace, and for Jerusalem's sake I will not rest, until the righteousness thereof go forth as brightness, and the salvation thereof as a lamp that burneth. And the Gentiles shall see thy righteousness, and all kings thy glory: and thou shalt be called by a new name, which the mouth of the LORD shall name... Son of man, I have made thee a watchman unto the house of Israel: therefore hear the word at my mouth, and give them warning from me" (Habakkuk 2:1-3; Luke 6:13; Isaiah 62:1-2, 7; Ezekiel 3:17).

The cardinal purpose of prayer watches is to pray unto God (Luke 6:12-13) and receive from Him (Habakkuk 2:1-2a). Thirdly, we pray and watch to hear clearly from God (Ezekiel 3:17) in order to speak to men in unmistakable terms. Fourthly, prayer watching is essential when you want to take key decisions in life and ministry (Luke 12:13). Fifthly, by observing prayer watches, Christian leadership will be able to receive divine perceptions of the struggles, hurts and crises of the membership (Matthew 14:23-25).

> ◈◈◈◈〇◈◈◈◈
> If we are sensitive to the leading and
> revelation of the Holy Spirit and
> acknowledge our entire dependence on God
> for guidance and empowerment, we would,
> no doubt, learn, love and practice prayer
> watches. If Jesus Christ did, we must.
> ◈◈◈◈〇◈◈◈◈

The sixth purpose of prayer watches is for revival praying that will usher in salvation, righteousness, glory and the praise of Jehovah God upon the earth. Seventhly; prayer watches enable us to fulfill our God-appointed ministries as watchmen, intercessions and royal priesthood (Ezekiel 3:17; 1 Timothy 2:1-4; 1 Peter 2:9). Finally, we engage the enemy in confrontational warfare to counter his manipulation and machinations (Matthew 13:25, 39; Judge 7:19).

Practice of Prayer Watches

> *"Arise, cry out in the night: in the beginning of the watches pour out thine heart like water before the face of the LORD: lift up thy hands toward him for the life of thy young children, that faint for hunger in the top of every street... So Gideon, and the hundred men that were with him, came unto the outside of the camp in the beginning of the middle watch; and they had but newly set the watch: and they blew the trumpets, and brake the pitchers that were in*

their hands... And in the fourth watch of the night Jesus went unto them, walking on the sea... For these are not drunken, as ye suppose, seeing it is but the third hour of the day... And Cornelius said, Four days ago I was fasting until this hour; and at the ninth hour I prayed in my house, and, behold, a man stood before me in bright clothing... When I remember thee upon my bed, and meditate on thee in the night watches" (Lamentations 2:19; Judges 7:19; Matthew 14:25; Acts 2:15; 10:30; Psalms 63:6; Read the following also: Habakkuk 2:1; Psalms 119:148; 1 Samuel 11:11; Exodus 14:24; Luke 12:37-38)

In both the Old and New Testaments, the practice of prayer watches was part of their spiritual discipline. The Old Testament saints practiced three segments or divisions of night watches - first watch (until midnight); middle watch (until 3.00 a.m.) and morning watch (until 6.00 a.m.). The ancient day watches were the morning (until about 10.00 a.m.); the heat of the day at about 2.00 p.m. and cool of the day (until 6.00 p.m.).

In the New Testament, night prayer watches were practiced in four divisions: first or evening watch (6.00 p.m. – 9.00 pm); second or midnight watch (9.00 p.m. – 12.00 p.m.); third or cockcrow (12.00 a.m. – 3.00 a.m.); fourth or morning watch (3.00 a.m. – 6.00 a.m.); the critical hours of night prayer watches were therefore 6.00 p.m., 9.00 p.m., 12.00 midnight and 3.00 a.m. In the day the apostolic fathers practiced hours of prayer: third hour (9.00 a.m.); sixth hour

(12.00 noon); ninth hour (3.00 p.m.) and twelfth hour (6.00 p.m.).

While we do not make a rigid doctrine out of prayer watches, the practice of prayer watches by our faith's apostolic forefathers explains their towering spiritual stature and our own spiritual dwarfism. They challenge us to give ourselves to prayer first.

> ❦❧❧❦❦❦**0**❦❦❦❦❧❧
> **The practice of prayer watches by our faith's apostolic forefathers explains their towering spiritual stature and our own spiritual dwarfism.**
> ❦❧❧❦❦❦**0**❦❦❦❦❧❧

Principles of Prayer Watches

There are principles that we must apply if we are to have effective prayer watches.

First principle: Decide to prayer-watch (Habakkuk 2:1). This step is crucial and everything begins and ends with it. For those who feel called to prayer and intercession, this decision is mandatory. After you have decided to prayer-watch you must also decide on the period (time) and place (Matthew 14:23; Luke 6:12; Mark 1:35).

Second principle: Define the purpose (Habakkuk 2:1). Prayer watches must not be a routine or done to just fulfil all righteousness as a spiritual obligation to enhance fellowship and walk with God and war against the enemy.

Third principle: Determine the pattern (Habakkuk. 2:1). The purpose will determine the pattern. If the purpose is for fellowship with God, the pattern of praise and worship will be adopted. Warfare will feature binding and loosing; and prayer watches for spiritual guidance will feature seeking, consecration and study. Prayer watches for revival will feature personal repentance, weeping, groaning, intercession and supplications (Isaiah 62:1-2, 6-7).

> ꙮ❦ꙮ **❶** ꙮ❦ꙮ
> Prayer watches must not be a routine or done to just fulfil all righteousness as a spiritual obligation to enhance fellowship and walk with God and war against the enemy.
> ꙮ❦ꙮ **❶** ꙮ❦ꙮ

Fourth principle: Be disciplined in your practice. (Daniel 10:2-3). Adequate preparation must be made in the day before the night of prayer watches will be effective. Over-indulgence of the appetite, over-working or excessive fatigue and talkativeness in the period preceding the prayer watches must be carefully avoided. It is particularly unhelpful to eat heavy meals before the prayer watches. We need to pray for effective time management also.

Fifth principle: Develop your perception (Habakkuk 2:1). To be refreshing and inspirational, prayer watches should not be a one-way communication process. We must learn to hear or discern what the Lord is saying to us at any particular time.

Sixth principle: Describe your perception (Habakkuk 2:2-3). Pen and papers must be handy. The Bible must be available for the process of reference and meditation. For future reference and utilization, it is important to record in a good exercise book or diary what appears to be God's dealing with you.

Seventh principle: Depend fully on God's power (Matthew 26:41; Zechariah 4:6). The enemy will do everything to hinder you from prayer watching. He knows that prayer watches will usher you into the glory of God (Luke 9:28-29) and bring the glory of God upon you (Exodus 34:30, 35). He knows you will receive power to fight against him and spoil his works. He will therefore move demonic opposition against you and weaken the effectiveness of your prayer watches (Luke 22:41-46). We must depend on the power of the Holy Ghost in order to be effective in our prayer watching.

The Challenges of Our Time

"The burden of Dumah. He calleth to me out of Seir, Watchman, what of the night? Watchman, what of the night?... Watch and pray, that ye enter not into temptation: the spirit indeed is willing, but the flesh is weak... And there arose a great storm of wind, and the waves beat into the ship, so that it was now full... And said unto them, Why sleep ye? rise and pray, lest ye

enter into temptation" (Isaiah 21:11; Mathew 26:41; Mark 4:37; Luke 22:46).

CHAPTER

9

꧁❀❀❀**0**❀❀❀꧂

PRAYER-BIRTHING
PROPHECIES

꧁❀❀❀**0**❀❀❀꧂

"In the first year of Darius the son of Ahasuerus, of the seed of the Medes, which was made king over the realm of the Chaldeans; In the first year of his reign I Daniel understood by books the number of the years, whereof the word of the LORD came to Jeremiah the prophet, that he would accomplish seventy years in the desolations of Jerusalem. And I set my face unto the Lord God, to seek by prayer and supplications, with fasting, and sackcloth, and ashes: And I prayed unto the LORD my God, and made my confession, and said, O Lord, the great and dreadful God, keeping the covenant and mercy to them that love him, and to them that keep his commandments... And this whole land shall be a desolation, and an astonishment; and these nations shall serve the king of Babylon seventy years. And it shall come to

pass, when seventy years are accomplished, that I will punish the king of Babylon, and that nation, saith the LORD, for their iniquity, and the land of the Chaldeans, and will make it perpetual desolations" (Daniel 9:1-4; Jeremiah 25:11-12; Read Jeremiah 29:1, 10-14; Isaiah 37:2-4).

THE gift of prophecy is the special ability that God gives to certain members of the Body of Christ to receive and communicate an immediate message from God to His people through a divinely anointed utterance. Prophecy involves fore-telling and forth-telling. It interprets the past and declares the future. (https://shepherdsofthelost.org)

The divinely anointed utterance becomes a prophetic word. Prophecy is the future revealed today. It is future history received and written today. It is the revelation of divine destiny. It is the communication of God's future dealings, purposes plans and programmes with man in the present.

Prophetic direction, words and revelation can be received through anointed activation of the written word, word of knowledge, visions, dreams, divine coincidence, irresistible urges, prophetic acts and uttered prayer pronouncements.

No true prophecy can go against God's will revealed in the Holy Scriptures. When God speaks good concerning our future or situation, it becomes a promissory note, that is, His divine intention and destiny for our lives. God says only what He would do and does exactly what He has said.

However, God's intentions must be prayer-birthed. Failure to prayer-birth withers personal or corporate prophecies. This is one of the reasons for their miscarriage leading to frustration and pain. God is, however, not to be blamed. You need to know the principles and practice of prayer-birthing prophecies.

> ❧❧❧❧❧ⓞ❧❧❧❧
> **No true prophecy can go against God's will revealed in the Holy Scriptures.**
> ❧❧❧❧ⓞ❧❧❧❧

Principles of Prayer-Birthing Prophecies

In Ezekiel Chapter 36, the principle of prayer-birthing prophecies is revealed. The prophecies concerning Israel's restoration can be categorized into seven-fold intentions of God.

i.   Ezekiel 36:1-12. Restoration of pleasant but impoverished places to plenty and prosperity

ii. Ezekiel 36:13-15. Restoration of the people from death and shame to life and honour.

iii. Ezekiel 6:16-24. Restoration of the people in captivity to freedom.

iv. Ezekiel 36:25-28. Restoration from defilement, depravity and desolation to salvation, sanctification and spirit-infilling.

v.   Ezekiel 36:29-30. Restoration from famine to fullness

vi. Ezekiel 36:33-35. Restoration from ruin to rest
vii. Ezekiel 36:38. Restoration from depopulation to appreciable population density.

Then Ezekiel 36:36b says: *"I the Lord have spoken it, and I will do it."* Where then does the principle of prayer-birthing this prophecy of restoration apply? It is in the first part of Ezekiel 36:37 *"Thus, says the Lord God, I WILL YET FOR THIS BE ENQUIRED OF BY THE HOUSE OF ISREAL, TO DO IT FOR THEM…."*

What could have happened if the people had failed to enquire of the Lord concerning this prophecy in all probability? Isaiah 37:3 says, *"And they said unto him, Thus saith Hezekiah, This day is a day of trouble, and of rebuke, and of blasphemy: for the children are come to the birth, and there is not strength to bring forth."* What could have been their experience? - unbirthed dreams, dashed hopes and unfulfilled expectations, of course!

"In the first year of Darius the son of Ahasuerus, of the seed of the Medes, which was made king over the realm of the Chaldeans; In the first year of his reign I Daniel understood by books the number of the years, whereof the word of the LORD came to Jeremiah the prophet, that he would accomplish seventy years in the desolations of Jerusalem. And I set my face unto the Lord God, to seek by prayer and supplications, with fasting, and sackcloth, and ashes: And I prayed unto the LORD my God, and made my confession, and said, O Lord, the great and dreadful God, keeping the covenant

and mercy to them that love him, and to them that keep his commandments... To fulfil the word of the LORD by the mouth of Jeremiah, until the land had enjoyed her sabbaths: for as long as she lay desolate she kept sabbath, to fulfil threescore and ten years. Now in the first year of Cyrus king of Persia, that the word of the LORD spoken by the mouth of Jeremiah might be accomplished, the LORD stirred up the spirit of Cyrus king of Persia, that he made a proclamation throughout all his kingdom, and put it also in writing, saying, Thus saith Cyrus king of Persia, All the kingdoms of the earth hath the LORD God of heaven given me; and he hath charged me to build him an house in Jerusalem, which is in Judah. Who is there among you of all his people? The LORD his God be with him, and let him go up" (Daniel 9:1-4; 2 Chronicles 36:21-23).

Daniel's prayer is a classic example of prayer-birthing prophecies. He prayer-birthed the fulfilment of Jeremiah's prophecy of the restoration of Israel from the Babylonian captivity. We see in his practice, the preliminary, the prayer birth and the prayer pattern.

i. **The Preliminary** - In Daniel 9:2 *"In the first year of his reign I Daniel understood by books the number of the years, whereof the word of the LORD came to Jeremiah the prophet, that he would accomplish seventy years in the desolations of Jerusalem."*

Three steps are vital here: (a) Receive the prophecy - *"whereof the word of the Lord came to Jeremiah the prophet"* (b) Record the prophecy - Jeremiah wrote down the prophecy in books which Daniel read later (c) Reflect on the prophecy – *"I understood by books the number of the years whereof the Lord spoke to Jeremiah."*

> ❧❧❧❧❧**0**❧❧❧❧❧
> Daniel's prayer is a classic example of prayer-birthing prophecies. He prayer-birthed the fulfilment of Jeremiah's prophecy of the restoration of Israel from the Babylonian captivity.
> ❧❧❧❧❧**0**❧❧❧❧❧

ii.   **The Prayer-birthing** - Daniel 9:3
There are four important steps to prayer-birthing here: (a) Set your face unto the Lord because the prophecy came from Him. (b) Seek the Lord by prayer for the fulfilment of His good word unto you and the averting of judgement. (c) Supplicate earnestly in prayer. Supplication is a passionate plea to God to do something about something. (d) Sanctify a fast.

iii.   **The Pattern** - Daniel 9:4-19; 10:1-3, 12
In Daniel's prayer, the following patterns are evident.

a. Commendation of God's faithfulness - Daniel 9:4; 1 Kings 9:5-6; Numbers 23:19; Joshua 21:45; 23:14; Hebrew 6:18.

b. Confession of personal and the people's failure and unfaithfulness. Sin and unfaithfulness abort God's prophecy and promise concerning any people or nation - Joshua 24:20.

c. Contents that revealed:
    i. Supplication - Daniel 9:8-10, 13-19
    ii. Acknowledgment of personal, public and parental failures - Daniel 9:5-20
    iii. Exaltation of God - Daniel 9:4, 7-8, 14-15
    iv. Contradistinction between God's faithfulness and Israel's unfaithfulness - Daniel 9:4-5, 7, 8-9
    v. The calling of a sin by its name as a sin - Daniel 9:6-10
    vi. He sanctified God - Daniel 9:4, 11-12
    vii. He accepted the punishment as well-deserved - Daniel 9:11-12
    viii. He owned God as theirs - Daniel 9:9-10,13-15,17
    ix. He made God's mercy, righteousness and name the strong points – Daniel 9:4, 7, 9
    x. He persisted for results – Daniel 10:2-3
    xi. He was bold – Daniel 10:19
    xii. He was urgent - Daniel 10:12

d. Confrontation with hindering principalities - Daniel 10:1-3, 13, 20

e.   Crying of groaning of labour pangs - Isaiah 37:3-4, 6; 6:7-8; Romans 8:26

f.   Comfort, confirmation and counsel from the throne of God - Daniel 9:20-24; 10:10-21.

CHAPTER

10

❧❧❧❧⓪❧❧❧❧

PRAYER WALKS
❧❧❧❧⓪❧❧❧❧

"Every place that the sole of your foot shall tread upon, that have I given unto you, as I said unto Moses... "(And I arose in the night, I and some few men with me; neither told I any man what my God had put in my heart to do at Jerusalem: neither was there any beast with me, save the beast that I rode upon. And I went out by night by the gate of the valley, even before the dragon well, and to the dung port, and viewed the walls of Jerusalem, which were broken down, and the gates thereof were consumed with fire. Then I went on to the gate of the fountain, and to the king's pool: but there was no place for the beast that was under me to pass. Then went I up in the night by the brook, and viewed the wall, and turned back, and entered by the gate of the valley, and so returned. And the rulers knew not whither I went, or what I did; neither had I as yet told it to the Jews, nor to the priests, nor to the nobles,

nor to the rulers, nor to the rest that did the work" (Joshua 1:3; Nehemiah 2:12-16).

PRAYER walk is an action prayer practice taken by believers who want to be God's end-time generals such as Joshua and Nehemiah. It is a practical prayer practice that answering the questions below will further clarify to know the what, who, why, how and when of this prayer principle.

What is Prayer Walking?

Prayer walking has been defined as praying on site with insight. It is the intercessory prayer offered in the very place you expect your prayer to be answered.

Who is a Prayer Walker?

A prayer walker is an unspotted believer in Christ who stands in the gap to intercede and supplicate on a defined geographical space to bring about the will of God for the harvest of souls in that delineated or designated area. He physically walks and navigates the entire land personally or in concert with other prayer walkers to spiritually uproot and displace prevailing satanic strongholds and rout the enemy.

Why do we Prayer-Walk?

We prayer-walk in order to exercise the dominion given to us by God (Joshua 1:3, Psalms 8:4-6; Mark 16:17-20; Acts 1:8). We prayer-walk to possess the gates of the enemy in out neighbourhood (Genesis 22:17; Psalms 27:5). We prayer-walk to bring down the wall between the church and the community.

We prayer-walk over our neighbourhood – streets, entry- points, schools, neighbours, hospitals, homes among others. Another reason for prayer walk is that in the process, we defuse satanic influence and power and bring the salvation of God, His glory and Kingdom into the neighbourhood.

> ༺ᏬᎦᏜᏜ❿ᏜᏜᏬᎦ༻
> A prayer walker is an unspotted believer in Christ who stands in the gap to intercede and supplicate on a defined geographical space to bring about the will of God for the harvest of souls in that delineated or designated area.
> ༺ᏬᎦᏜᏜ❿ᏜᏜᏬᎦ༻

Where do we Prayer Walk?

i. A Christian student/teacher can prayer-walk his/her school praying for the students, teachers and workers
ii. An executive/worker can prayer-walk his/her office
iii. A Christian doctor, nurse, pharmacist and other hospital workers can prayer-walk the hospital, pharmacy, infirmary, health centre or clinic
iv. The trader can prayer-walk the market
v. The main entry points to the church, community or school can be prayer-walked

vi.   The streets, parks, hotels, church environment, residential blocks and worship locations can all be prayer-walked. Believers can prayer-walk to the service.

How do we Prayer Walk?

It must be pointed out that the term prayer-walking does not necessarily imply, as it supposedly conveys, the idea of being in perpetual motion while praying.

The essence is that you are on site praying with insight. The following steps are suggested for effective prayer walking.

i.   Mark out the site to prayer-walk bearing number three above in mind.

ii.   Map out the spiritual geography of the site to be prayer-walked. Spiritual geography simply means seeing your community as God sees it. You map out the spiritual stronghold, strongman and dynamics of the neighbourhood.

iii.   Make up a team of two, three or more

iv.   Maintain a schedule, for example, starting with one prayer-walk a week, a month, a quarter, a half year or yearly.

v.   Meet, if necessary (especially if the prayer walk is organized) after the exercise, to share your experiences and map out new strategies.

vi.   Maintain link with the Holy Ghost for adequate insight even while on site.

Are there any Spiritual Dangers in Prayer Walking?

None, except when there is an Achan in the camp (Joshua 7).

What are the Benefits of Prayer Walks?

i. The wall between the church and the community is broken down
ii. The enemy's power is broken and his influence neutralised
iii. The believer learns action-praying
iv. Spiritual blessings: Salvation, righteousness and divine protection are brought into the neighbourhood among others.

It must be pointed out that the term prayer-walking does not necessarily imply, as it supposedly conveys, the idea of being in perpetual motion while praying.

CHAPTER

11

≪∾≈∾⊚∾≈∾≫
CORPORATE PRAYING
≪∾≈∾⊚∾≈∾≫

"These all continued with one accord in prayer and supplication, with the women, and Mary the mother of Jesus, and with his brethren... And they continued stedfastly in the apostles' doctrine and fellowship, and in breaking of bread, and in prayers... Peter therefore was kept in prison: but prayer was made without ceasing of the church unto God for him... Again I say unto you, That if two of you shall agree on earth as touching any thing that they shall ask, it shall be done for them of my Father which is in heaven" (Acts 1:14; 2:42; 12:5; Matthew 18:19; also read Deuteronomy 32:30; Acts 4:23-31).

CORPORATE praying is any prayer activity which involves more than one person. It could be held in a family, church service, among prayer warriors, at specially scheduled prayer workshops, seminars, night vigils, morning prayers and prayer watches. The Scripture is full of examples of powerful corporate praying (2 Chronicles 20:1-20; Acts 4:23-31).

When the apostolic believers prayed, people, places and powers were shaken by the tremors of their prayer fire-power. When they prayed, the Pharisees were in trouble and iron gates were broken. What is the trouble with today's corporate prayer meetings and what tips can make them potent?

> When the apostolic believers prayed, people, places and powers were shaken by the tremors of their prayer fire-power. When they prayed, the Pharisees were in trouble and iron gates were broken.

Problems with Corporate Prayer Meetings

i.   Lack of unity. *"Behold, how good and how pleasant it is for brethren to dwell together in unity! It is like the precious ointment upon the head, that ran down upon the beard, even Aaron's beard: that went down to the skirts of his garments; As the dew of Hermon, and as the dew that descended upon the mountains of Zion: for there the LORD commanded the blessing, even life for evermore"* (Psalms 133:1-3; Read Acts 1:14; 2:42; 4:22-23).

ii.   The meetings are boring – Psalms 74:9

iii.   Lack of individual involvement. *"And being let go, they went to their own company, and reported all that the chief priests and elders had said unto them"* (Acts 4:23).

iv.   Prayer meetings have become another preaching time of taking participants on guilt-trip

v.   Prayer meeting have become another gossip group

vi.   No answers to show - no testimonies to give after a successful prayer meeting

vii.   No demonstration or manifestation of the presence and power of the Holy Ghost and the spirit of worship. In Acts. 4:31, *"And when they had prayed, the place was shaken where they were assembled together; and they were all filled with the Holy Ghost, and they spake the word of God with boldness."*

Steps to Effective Corporate Praying

A number of factors that contribute to effective corporate praying include the following:

1.   The pastor and older believers. In Acts 2:43-44; 6:4. They must attend corporate prayer meetings, pray effectively and show verbally to the younger believers and new comers, models in praying.

2.   The corporate prayer leaders. Those who come to lead corporate prayers must pray effectively and efficiently in private – Matthew 6:5-6.

3.   The sequence of calling out our prayer items. This must not be punctuated by little sermons which divert the flow of corporate praying.

4.   Worship. A spirit of worship, praise and thanksgiving must saturate corporate praying. Psalms 149, 150

5. Concert prayer. Acts 4:22-23. This means that participants and leaders must pray out loud at the same time or that all agree with the prayer of the prayer leader. Silence is one way of "killing the power" of corporate prayers.

6. Specificity of prayer items - Acts 4:24-30. Generalized prayer request may leave people in doubt of what to pray to for.

7. Effectiveness of the prayer. Act 12:5-12; 4:31-32. Corporate prayer must show evidence there must be results to show for them.

8. Hearing God. Corporate prayer meetings where participant sense God speaking to exhort, edify, equip, energize and encourage cannot but be powerful.

The sequence of calling out our prayer items. This must not be punctuated by little sermons which divert the flow of corporate praying.

CHAPTER

12

꒰꒱꒰꒱**0**꒰꒱꒰꒱

PRAISE MARCHES

꒰꒱꒰꒱**0**꒰꒱꒰꒱

"How beautiful upon the mountains are the feet of him that bringeth good tidings, that publisheth peace; that bringeth good tidings of good, that publisheth salvation; that saith unto Zion, Thy God reigneth! Thy watchmen shall lift up the voice; with the voice together shall they sing: for they shall see eye to eye, when the LORD *shall bring again Zion. Break forth into joy, sing together, ye waste places of Jerusalem: for the* LORD *hath comforted his people, he hath redeemed Jerusalem. The* LORD *hath made bare his holy arm in the eyes of all the nations; and all the ends of the earth shall see the salvation of our God"* (Isaiah 52:7-10; Read Joshua 6).

WE generally associate marches with armies. The body of Christ is an army. We are to march for Jesus with our feet. Isaiah exclaims, *"How beautiful upon the mountains are the of him that bringeth tidings that publish peace, that bringeth good tidings of sound, that published salvation; that saith unto Zion, Thy God reigneth.!"* (Isaiah 52:7)

Purpose of Praise Marches

"Behind the doors also and the posts hast thou set up thy remembrance: for thou hast discovered thyself to another than me, and art gone up; thou hast enlarged thy bed, and made thee a covenant with them; thou lovedst their bed where thou sawest it. And thou wentest to the king with ointment, and didst increase thy perfumes, and didst send thy messengers far off, and didst debase thyself even unto hell. Thou art wearied in the greatness of thy way; yet saidst thou not, There is no hope: thou hast found the life of thine hand; therefore thou wast not grieved." (Isaiah 57:8-10).

The main purpose of praise marches is for the whole body of Christ to proclaim public worship of the Lordship of Jesus. Indirectly, the Church brings good tidings and publishes peace and salvation to the city where praise marches are carried out. The purpose of Jesus March is to bring the whole Body of Christ to the agreement of giving public praise to God.

Power of Praise Marches

"Enter into his gates with thanksgiving, and into his courts with praise: be thankful unto

him, and bless his name... Let the saints be joyful in glory: let them sing aloud upon their beds. Let the high praises of God be in their mouth, and a two-edged sword in their hand; To execute vengeance upon the heathen, and punishments upon the people; To bind their kings with chains, and their nobles with fetters of iron; To execute upon them the judgement written: this honour have all his saints. Praise ye the Lord... And at midnight Paul and Silas prayed, and sang praises unto God: and the prisoners heard them. And suddenly there was a great earthquake, so that the foundations of the prison were shaken: and immediately all the doors were opened, and every one's bands were loosed" (Psalms 100:4, 149:5-9; Acts 16:25-26; Please read 2 Chronicles 5:11-14; 20:21-28).

Praise releases the power of God whereby locked doors are opened, sealed gates are broken, captives are freed and battles are won. Moreover, God inhabits the praise of His people. His glory is revealed when we praise Him.

Practice of Praise

God must be worshipped in truth and in spirit. The worship in general sense refers to as giving honour to God with prayers, praise, and bringing our sacrificial gifts. *"And this man went up out of his city yearly to worship and to sacrifice unto the LORD of hosts in Shiloh. And the two sons of Eli, Hophni and Phinehas, the priests of the LORD, were there"* (1 Samuel

1:3). In a narrow sense, worship in pure adoration unto the Lord.

> ❧❧❦❧❶❧❦❧❧❧
> **Praise releases the power of God whereby locked doors are opened, sealed gates are broken, captives are freed and battles are won.**
> ❧❧❦❧❶❧❦❧❧❧

The Bible reveals that praise can be practiced in the following forms:

i.   Clapping (Psalms 47:1)
ii. Joyful noise (Psalms 95:1)
iii. Leaping (Luke 6:23; Acts 3:8)
iv. Shouting (Psalms 47:1; 1 Thessalonians 4:16)
v.   Lifting hands (Psalms 63:4; 134:2; 1 Timothy 2:8)
vi. Bowing down and kneeling (Psalms 95:6)
vii. Dancing (Psalms 150:4; Ecclesiastes 3:4; Exodus 15:20; Psalms 30:11; 150:4; Luke 15:25)
viii. Marching (Judges 5:4; 2 Chronicles 20:20-25)
ix. Music accompanied by playing of musical instruments (2 Samuel 6:5; 1 Chronicles 25:1-7; 2 Kings 3:15; Psalms 150; Ephesians 5:19)
x.   Singing (1 Chronicles 9:27-33; Isaiah e38:18-20; Colossians 3:16)

The praise practised will determine the kind of praise to be offered. For example:

i. Today, praise is practised by a choir of worshippers. 1 Chronicles 25:1-7. However, it is instructive that every believer practises praise.

ii. In Barak praise, you kneel to bless God in adoration. Psalms 95:6

iii. In Shabach praise, you "shout, to address in a loud tone, to command, to triumph." You praise God with a might shout. Psalms 47:1

iv. In Samar praise, musical instrument is used to praise God. Psalms 150:3-5

v. In Halal praise, from which Halleluiah is derived, you celebrate the Lord. Isaiah 38:18

vi. Tehillah praise is more like a hymn or a laudation. "the singing of halals, to sing or to laud; perceived to involve music, especially singing hymns of the Spirit or praise." (https://www.aglow.org).

vii. Hymns. *"Speaking to yourselves in Psalms and hymns and spiritual songs, singing and making melody in your heart to the Lord; Giving thanks always for all things unto God and the Father in the name of our Lord Jesus Christ; Submitting yourselves one to another in the fear of God"* (Ephesians 5:19-21).

Principles of Praise Marches

For effective praise marches or what is popularly called *March for Jesus*, the following must be included:

i. A clear delineation of the route of the march indicating starting and finishing points

ii. Obedience on the part of the Church of God's desire to worship Him

iii. Visibility of the Church

iv.   Unity of the Church

v.   Confession, repentance and reconciliation

vi.   Proclamation of Jesus only

vii.   Celebration. The march must be carried out in a festive mood with jubilation

viii.   Prophetic symbolism of Old Testament leadership

ix.   Boldness to preach the Gospel

x.   Claiming grounds. *"Every place that the sole of your foot shall tread upon, that have I given unto you, as I said unto Moses"* (Joshua 1:3).

xi.   Witness into the heavenly realm.

CHAPTER

13

❧❧❧❧**0**❧❧❧❧

PRAYER ACTIONS FOR
END-TIME GENERALS

❧❧❧❧**0**❧❧❧❧

Jeremiah 9:12-14, 17-20, 23-24 says;

"Who is the wise man, that may understand this? and who is he to whom the mouth of the LORD hath spoken, that he may declare it, for what the land perisheth and is burned up like a wilderness, that none passeth through? And the LORD saith, Because they have forsaken my law which I set before them, and have not obeyed my voice, neither walked therein; But have walked after the imagination of their own heart, and after Baalim, which their fathers taught them... Thus saith the LORD of hosts, Consider ye, and call for the mourning women, that they may come; and send for cunning women, that they may come: And let them make haste, and take up a wailing for us, that our eyes may run down

with tears, and our eyelids gush out with waters. For a voice of wailing is heard out of Zion, How are we spoiled! we are greatly confounded, because we have forsaken the land, because our dwellings have cast us out. Yet hear the word of the LORD, O ye women, and let your ear receive the word of his mouth, and teach your daughters wailing, and every one her neighbour lamentation... Thus saith the LORD, Let not the wise man glory in his wisdom, neither let the mighty man glory in his might, let not the rich man glory in his riches: But let him that glorieth glory in this, that he understandeth and knoweth me, that I am the LORD which exercise lovingkindness, judgement, and righteousness, in the earth: for in these things I delight, saith the LORD."

P RAYER expeditions and prayer journeys are two advanced actions research for the stout-hearted who have been called and commissioned by the Almighty God to open up an area to the Kingdom of God and to track and destroy the strongholds of the enemy. These are known as spiritual or end-time generals who are at the command of the Master, Commander-in-Chief and Generalissimo of the Forces of Righteousness.

Prayer Expeditions

"For though we walk in the flesh, we do not war after the flesh: (For the weapons of our warfare are not carnal, but mighty through God

to the pulling down of strong holds;) Casting down imaginations, and every high thing that exalteth itself against the knowledge of God, and bringing into captivity every thought to the obedience of Christ; And having in a readiness to revenge all disobedience, when your obedience is fulfilled...Blessed is the man whose strength is in thee; in whose heart are the ways of them. Who passing through the valley of Baca make it a well; the rain also filleth the pools" (Psalms 84:5-6).

While prayer walks focus on neighbourhoods, praise marches target cities, prayer expeditions trail territories or regions. The purpose of a prayer expedition is 'to open a given region spiritually to the Kingdom of God.' Prayer expedition is for the matured, committed, experienced and gifted believer with reasonable competence in strategic-level spiritual warfare - Ephesians 6:12.

> ꧁ ☙☙☙☙**0**☙☙☙☙ ꧂
>
> Prayer expeditions and prayer journeys are for the stout-hearted who have been called and commissioned by the Almighty God to open up an area to the Kingdom of God and to track and destroy the strongholds of the enemy. These are known as spiritual or end-time generals who are at the command of the Master, Commander-in-Chief and Generalissimo of the Forces of Righteousness.
>
> ꧁ ☙☙☙☙**0**☙☙☙☙ ꧂

To be effective, prayer expedition needs a reasonable level of knowledge of spiritual reading. This is an attempt to describe the regions as it really is and not as it appears to be. The spiritual geography of a region, state or territory will also reveal its potentials for redemptive benefits.

A city's redemptive gifts are those divine endowments bestowed upon a city to be used for contribution to the Kingdom of God. During prayer expeditions, satan's strongholds are discerned and destroyed to usher in the Kingdom of God. Peter Wagner has listed four keys of pray items during prayer expeditions:

(i)   Prayer of Repentance – 2 Chronicles 7:14
(ii)   Prayer of Intercession – Ezekiel 22:30
(iii)   Prayer of Proclamation – Psalms 86:8-9
(iv)   Prayer of Blessing – Deuteronomy 28:3-13

It should be noted that when Moses interceded for Israel, Aaron stood between the dead and the living – *"And he stood between the dead and the living; and the plague was stayed."* (Numbers 16:48)

Prayer Journeys

"But as for me, my prayer is unto thee, O LORD, in an acceptable time: O God, in the multitude of thy mercy hear me, in the truth of thy salvation…For though we walk in the flesh, we do not war after the flesh: (For the weapons of our warfare are not carnal, but mighty through God to the pulling down of strong

holds;) Casting down imaginations, and every high thing that exalteth itself against the knowledge of God, and bringing into captivity every thought to the obedience of Christ" (Psalms 69:13; 2 Corinthians 10:3-5).

While prayer walks focus on neighbourhoods, praise marches target cities, prayer expeditions trail territories or regions. The purpose of a prayer expedition is 'to open a given region spiritually to the Kingdom of God.'

While prayer walks focus on neighborhoods, praise marches on cities, prayer expeditions on regions; the primary domain of prayer journeys is on strongholds. Paul mentioned four strongholds.

i.   Sectarian or ideological stronghold – imaginations
ii. Occultic stronghold – every high thing that exalts itself against God
iii. Stronghold of the mind – bringing every thought into captivity
iv. Personal stronghold – opposed to the obedience of Christ

There are basically two types of prayer journey – (Excerpt from Peter Wagner).

(i)   **Intercessory prayer journeys** where a given church or ministry sends a prayer team to another city/country or certain strategic locations for the purpose of praying on site.

(ii)   **Prophetic prayer journeys.** Here "prophetic prayer actions are done only at the Lord's command in God's perfect timing according to a strategy that the Lord has revealed to the team" (Peter Wagner).

As we stand on the threshold of the 21st century, God's Spirit will be militarized on the Body of Christ to action prayers that will change the world.

Praying Until your Miracles Come

"For Zion's sake will I not hold my peace, and for Jerusalem's sake I will not rest, until the righteousness thereof go forth as brightness, and the salvation thereof as a lamp that burneth. And the Gentiles shall see thy righteousness, and all kings thy glory: and thou shalt be called by a new name, which the mouth of the LORD shall name. Thou shalt also be a crown of glory in the hand of the LORD, and a royal diadem in the hand of thy God... I have set watchmen upon thy walls, O Jerusalem, which shall never hold their peace day nor night: ye that make mention of the LORD, keep not silence, And give him no rest, till he establish, and till he make Jerusalem a praise in the earth" (Isaiah 62:1-3, 6-7; Also, read Luke 11:5-13).

In the end-time, God's generals will consist of men, women and youths who will appropriate and discern the will of God for them and hold unto the throne until they see the fulfilment of that divine destiny. Like Jacob, they will wrestle in prayer until God blesses them and changes them to spiritual princes and princesses.

As Jabez, God's generals will pray until prayer turns their sorrow into joy. They will give God no rest, day or night, until their salvation (deliverance) rest and righteousness go forth as the brightness of a burning lamp. *"For Zion's sake will I not hold my peace, and for Jerusalem's sake I will not rest, until the righteousness thereof go forth as brightness, and the salvation thereof as a lamp that burneth"* (Isaiah 62:1).

Holding-on Principles

"And he said unto them, Which of you shall have a friend, and shall go unto him at midnight, and say unto him, Friend, lend me three loaves; For a friend of mine in his journey is come to me, and I have nothing to set before him? And he from within shall answer and say, Trouble me not: the door is now shut, and my children are with me in bed; I cannot rise and give thee. I say unto you, Though he will not rise and give him, because he is his friend, yet because of his importunity he will rise and give him as many as he needeth. And I say unto you, Ask, and it shall be given you; seek, and ye shall find; knock, and it shall be opened unto you. For every one that asketh receiveth; and he

that seeketh findeth; and to him that knocketh it shall be opened. If a son shall ask bread of any of you that is a father, will he give him a stone? or if he ask a fish, will he for a fish give him a serpent? Or if he shall ask an egg, will he offer him a scorpion? If ye then, being evil, know how to give good gifts unto your children: how much more shall your heavenly Father give the Holy Spirit to them that ask him?" (Luke 11:5-13).

i.   Know your need. Luke 11:5 - Lend me three loaves.

ii. Know your source. Luke 11:5 – Friend, lend me three loaves. God is a source and Jesus is our friend.

iii. Have courage or boldness before the throne. Luke 11:5. Which of you shall have a friend and shall go to him at MIDNIGHT? Hebrews 4:16.

iv. Have a persistent or prevailing spirit. Luke 11:8 - Yet because of his importunity he will rise and give him.

v.   Stay on the throne until your miracles come Luke 11:8 - He will rise and give him as many as he needeth.

vi. When you seek and do not receive, do not give up; go the next mile - seek - Luke 11:9; Jeremiah 29:12-14.

vii. When you seek and do not seem to find, then knock and the door will be opened unto you – Matthew 7:7.

Note: Asking implies want; seeking implies desire and knocking implies need. To pray until your miracles come implies that you must ask with humility and confidence, seek with care and application; and knock with earnestness, perseverance and holy desperation.

viii.   Have faith God will give you your miracles - Luke 11:10-13.

CHAPTER

14

❧❧❧❧⓿❧❧❧❧

AARON AND HUR SUPPORTIVE MINISTRY

❧❧❧❧⓿❧❧❧❧

Exodus 17:8-16 says, *"Then came Amalek, and fought with Israel in Rephidim. And Moses said unto Joshua, Choose us out men, and go out, fight with Amalek: to morrow I will stand on the top of the hill with the rod of God in mine hand. So Joshua did as Moses had said to him, and fought with Amalek: and Moses, Aaron, and Hur went up to the top of the hill. And it came to pass, when Moses held up his hand, that Israel prevailed: and when he let down his hand, Amalek prevailed. But Moses hands were heavy; and they took a stone, and put it under him, and he sat thereon; and Aaron and Hur stayed up his hands, the one on the one side, and the other on the other side; and his hands were steady until the going down of the sun. And Joshua discomfited Amalek and his people with the edge of the sword. And the LORD said unto Moses, Write this for a memorial in a book, and rehearse it in the ears of Joshua: for I will utterly put out the remembrance of Amalek from under heaven. And Moses built an altar, and called the name of it Jehovah Nissi: For he said, Because the LORD hath sworn that the LORD will have war with Amalek from generation to generation."*

NEW Testament churches must employ the principle of Aaron and Hur for a successful ministry and to enhance the proclamation of the gospel of Christ on earth. All leaders and their families and ministries need to be surrounded by a shield of prayer as it is important to understand that role as they constantly remain the target of the devil.

Even if you are not called into a unique role as a personal intercessor for your pastor, you can still pray faithfully for your leaders, whether you have a special assignment or not.

Many leaders need the Aarons and Hurs to rise up and hold up their arms in the prayer of intercession and supplications. Leaders are like Generals in God's army and Satan's attacks are aimed directly at them. Their callings, works, marriages and ministries are the target of the devil and his cohorts because satan, a defeated foe, is always antagonistic to the work of Christ on earth. We often hear of leaders' errors and mistakes. Some lose their emotional, mental or physical health due to stress and attacks while a number also fell from grace to grass.

> ༚ॐ࿐᠅᠑**0**᠑᠅࿐ॐ༚
> Leaders are like Generals in God's army
> and Satan's attacks are aimed directly at
> them. Their callings, works, marriages
> and ministries are the target of the devil
> and his cohorts ... We often hear of
> leaders' errors and mistakes. Some lose
> their emotional, mental or physical health
> due to stress and attacks while a number
> also fell from grace to grass.
> ༚ॐ࿐᠅᠑**0**᠑᠅࿐ॐ༚

"For a bishop must be blameless, as the steward of God; not selfwilled, not soon angry, not given to wine, no striker, not given to filthy lucre; But a lover of hospitality, a lover of good men, sober, just, holy, temperate; Holding fast the faithful word as he hath been taught, that he may be able by sound doctrine both to exhort and to convince the gainsayers" (Titus 1:7–9).

The power of teamwork or three-fold cord are not easily broken – this comprises of Moses' raised staff of warfare on the Amalekites, Aaron and Hur's back-up and Joshua's all-out fighting the battle brought about a sustainable prevailing victory over the enemy of God. Aaron was the priest and main helper of Moses while Hur held no special office but joined in the battle for truth. The power of three-in-one won the victory against the Amalekites.

In church ministry, we also need such teamwork if we want healthy leaders and church members prepared for Christ's second coming. We are on the battle field. As Moses needed Aaron and Hur, so also the Church leaders need their co-workers and members to join them in fighting the invisible battle for a successful ministry.

> *"But now are they many members, yet but one body. And the eye cannot say unto the hand, I have no need of thee: nor again the head to the feet, I have no need of you. Nay, much more those members of the body, which seem to be more feeble, are necessary"* (1 Corinthians 12:20-22).

Aaron and Hur principle is God's best strategy to defeat the Amalekites - they were united in one accord in prayers and supplications.

> *"Also the sons of the stranger, that join themselves to the Lord, to serve him, and to love the name of the Lord, to be his servants, every one that keepeth the sabbath from polluting it, and taketh hold of my covenant; Even them will I bring to my holy mountain, and make them joyful in my house of prayer: their burnt offerings and their sacrifices shall be accepted upon mine altar; for mine house shall be called an house of prayer for all people"* (Isaiah 56:6-7).

The body of believers must use the power and practice of prayer to combat spiritual warfare and demobilize the forces of darkness to pave way for the salvation of souls and preservation of believers; and to cultivate a close and personal relationship with God.

Also, the prayer for leaders must include that they and their families should be delivered from every evil work and that they be equipped with divine strength to fight the good fight of faith for great exploits and expansion of Christ's Kingdom.

Furthermore, that they may pursue righteousness, holiness, godliness, faith, love, mercy, endurance, gentleness, get prepared for every good work and remain spotless in spirit, soul and body up until the appearance of our soon-returning Savior.

CHAPTER

15

৵৽৾৽ৡ**0**ৡ৾৽৵৽

FAITH FOR FRUITFULNESS IN GOD'S SERVICE

৵৽৾৽ৡ**0**ৡ৾৽৵৽

"Ye have not chosen me, but I have chosen you, and ordained you, that ye should go and bring forth fruit, and that your fruit should remain: that whatsoever ye shall ask of the Father in my name, he may give it you...But without faith it is impossible to please him: for he that cometh to God must believe that he is, and that he is a rewarder of them that diligently seek him" (John 15:16; Hebrew 11:6).

GOD called and commissioned us to serve in His Kingdom with a measure of grace and talents given to everyone. He is a purpose-driven investor Who waits and watches for returns with dividends. He has the foreknowledge of all things and all that should be done to ensure success.

God expects no failure from us as He never fails. This is the reason Christ says, *"I have chosen you, and ordained you, that ye should go and bring fruit, and that your fruit should remain..."* God is ever ready to wind up His dealings with the fruitless believer and give more grace to the believer who brings Him returns on His investment. In John 15:2 and Luke 13:6-9;

> *"Every branch in me that beareth not fruit he taketh away: and every branch that beareth fruit, he purgeth it, that it may bring forth more fruit... He spake also this parable; A certain man had a fig tree planted in his vineyard; and he came and sought fruit thereon, and found none. Then said he unto the dresser of his vineyard, Behold, these three years I come seeking fruit on this fig tree, and find none: cut it down; why cumbereth it the ground? And he answering said unto him, Lord, let it alone this year also, till I shall dig about it, and dung it: And if it bear fruit, well: and if not, then after that thou shalt cut it down."*

There is no permanent column for failure in God's economy. Bad investments are wound up after some period of extended grace. We are God's investment - God's husbandry, set in a very "fruitful hill, ...fenced and planted with the choicest vine," watched and watered by the Holy Spirit (Isaiah 5:2).

Do we have any reason to fail to reproduce or bear the fruit of holy living, soul-winning and saintly service unto God? *"What could have been done more to my vineyard, that I have not done in it? wherefore, when I looked that it should bring forth grapes, brought it forth wild grapes?"* (Isaiah 5:4).

> ❧❧❧❧❧**O**❧❧❧❧❧
> There is no permanent column for
> failure in God's economy. Bad
> investments are wound up after some
> period of extended grace. We are
> God's investment - God's husbandry,
> set in a very "fruitful hill,
> ❧❧❧❧**O**❧❧❧❧❧

Jesus saved us and brought us into His Kingdom to receive nourishment and sustenance by the most holy faith. We are fed by pure milk of the word to build up, grow with the Spirit power and still growing. Therefore, we have all the basic requirements for fruitfulness in service and there is no reason for failure.

Faith for Fruitful Service

"If any of you lack wisdom, let him ask of God, that giveth to all men liberally, and upbraideth not; and it shall be given him. But let him ask in faith, nothing wavering. For he that wavereth is like a wave of the sea driven with the wind and tossed. For let not that man think that he shall receive any thing of the Lord. A double minded man is unstable in all his ways... Be sober, be vigilant; because your adversary the devil, as a roaring lion, walketh about, seeking whom he may devour: Whom resist stedfast in the faith, knowing that the same afflictions are accomplished in your brethren that are in the

world..." (James 1:5-8; 1 Peter 5:8-9; Read Hebrews 11:6-37).

Faith is the foundation of our relationship with God. We are saved by grace through faith, *"For by grace are ye saved through faith; and that not of yourselves: it is the gift of God: Not of works, lest any man should boast"* Ephesians 2:8-9). We are chosen and appointed by faith. The Christian service device runs exclusively on the battery of faith. We are serving the Lord Whom we have never seen. Yet, we believe He has sent us by the power of His Spirit; and He is taking stock and preparing a dividend sheet.

By faith, we seek His help when: the going gets tough, temptation is rife, the devil and his cohorts loom in view, our strength dips, the fields are hard, the sinners are stubborn and saints begin questioning.

> ❧❧❧❀𝟎❀❧❧❧
> **The Christian service device runs exclusively on the battery of faith.**
> ❧❧❧❀𝟎❀❧❧❧

In our dealings with God and our journey along the narrow way, it is impossible to have a hot and consistent way of righteousness without faith. We will soon imagine the beckoning of Jezebel's delicate fingers and her poisonous lips dropping honeycombs. We will soon begin to question the wisdom in our obedience, sacrifice and loyalty. Without faith, we can do or get nothing.

It's by faith we fight the invisible war in the Lord's name and prevail. Also by faith, we move God to stop the sun, hold the moon and bar the sky until we have gathered in the sheaves. Without faith, we can't please God and bear fruit. Who wants to bear the fruit of Christian service and holy living? Let him have faith in God, practice faith in God and live by it. For *"all things are possible to him that believeth"* (Mark 9:23).

Faithfulness for Fruitful Service

"Let a man so account of us, as of the ministers of Christ, and stewards of the mysteries of God. Moreover, it is required in stewards, that a man be found faithful...He said therefore, A certain nobleman went into a far country to receive for himself a kingdom, and to return. And he called his ten servants, and delivered them ten pounds, and said unto them, Occupy till I come...The burden of Dumah. He calleth to me out of Seir, Watchman, what of the night? Watchman, what of the night? The watchman said, The morning cometh, and also the night: if ye will enquire, enquire ye: return, come...Holding fast the faithful word as he hath been taught, that he may be able by sound doctrine both to exhort and to convince the gainsayers" (1 Corinthians 4:1-2; Luke 19:12-13; Isaiah 21:11-12; Titus 1:9).

Faithfulness is necessary for fruitfulness. It relates to firmness in pursuit of divine goals. It's steadfastness in the performance of letter and spirit to fulfilling divine order. Faithfulness glues the believer to his call and ministry with the tenacity of conviction, commitment, purpose and practice. The faithful does not waiver, cringe or recant. His heart is fixed, firm in his confession and unmovable is his conviction. He is ready to die on duty.

A planted seed germinates, grows up and bears fruit because it receives rain and nutrients consistently. So also is the fruit-bearing Christian in the presence of God. The faithful Christian is undeterred by affliction, persecution, want and initial failures. He holds fast that which the Lord has given him and labours in hope.

> The faithful does not waiver, cringe or recant. His heart is fixed, firm in his confession and unmovable is his conviction. He is ready to die on duty.

Desiring Eternal Praise

"Fear not, little flock; for it is your Father's good pleasure to give you the kingdom... His lord said unto him, Well done, thou good and faithful servant: thou hast been faithful over a few things, I will make thee ruler over many things: enter thou into the joy of thy lord... Now all these things happened unto them for examples: and they are written for our admonition, upon whom the ends of the world are come. Wherefore let him that thinketh he standeth take heed lest he fall. There hath no

temptation taken you but such as is common to man: but God is faithful, who will not suffer you to be tempted above that ye are able; but will with the temptation also make a way to escape, that ye may be able to bear it" (Luke 12:32; Matthew 25:21; 2 Corinthians 10:11-13; Read Matthew 7:21-25).

The fearful records of those who seemed to be productive in ministry as a whole but missed the Kingdom of Heaven call us to take heed and avoid their pitfalls. See their tragic list:

a.   The young prophet (1 Kings 13:20-24). It is possible for older believers or leaders to give counsel or guidance that appears to be from the Lord but is not actually from Him. This is the reason such a Christian must study the Bible regularly to know what God is saying on a particular issue. The young prophet let down his spiritual sensitivity and guard and was deceived.

b.   Balaam and Demas (Numbers 22:15-17; 2 Timothy 4:10) Love of popularity, promotion and prosperity.

c.   Judas Iscariot and Gehazi were both covetous (Matthew 24:14-16; 2 Kings 5:26-27).

d.   King Saul missed it because of the fear of man and attempt to please everybody. (1 Samuel 15:24).

Such examples of tragic figures are not to frighten but to warn us of the conditional nature of our salvation and to condition our minds to make eternal life our priority.

Labouring in the Kingdom of God is likened to running a race; only the winner gets the prize.

We must, like Paul, run not as one that beats the air but must keep under our body to excel and escape the possibility of being a castaway (1 Corinthians 9:27). Every Christian is called firstly to a life of fellowship with Christ and then to fruitful service either as a prayer warrior or minister. From the scriptures, we find out that our call is a call to:

- Sonship, saintliness and service
- Friendship, fellowship and fruitfulness
- Separation, suffering (for the faith) and splendour
- Followership, faithfulness and fullness
- Sheepfold, shepherding, supplication and intercession
- Humility, holiness and heaven-mindedness.

Our God is well able to keep us from falling because it's His delight to give us the Kingdom. We must obey the word of God, watch, pray and walk worthy of God and of our vocation.

≈❧☙⤏❀**0**❀⤎❧☙≈
QUOTABLE QUOTES ON PRAYERS
≈❧☙⤏❀**0**❀⤎❧☙≈

"And Moses cried unto the Lord, saying, Heal her now, O God, I beseech thee"

– Numbers 12:13

"God is looking for people to use, and if you can get usable, he will wear you out. The most dangerous prayer you can pray is this: 'Use me.'"

- Rick Warren

"Intercessory prayer is an act of communion with Christ, for Jesus pleads for the sons of men."

- Charles Spurgeon

"Intercession is the truly universal work for the Christian. No place is closed to intercessory prayer: no continent, no nation, no city, no organization, no office. No power on earth can keep intercession out"

- Richard Halverson

"God shapes the world by prayer. The more praying there is in the world the better the world will be, the mightier the forces against evil."

- Mother Teresa

"The Church has not yet touched the fringe of the possibilities of intercessory prayer. Her largest victories will be witnessed when individual Christians everywhere come to recognize their priesthood unto God and day by day give themselves unto prayer."

- John Mott

"Intercessory prayer is exceedingly prevalent. What wonders it has wrought! The Word of God teems with its marvelous deeds. Believer, thou hast a mighty engine in thy hand, use it well, use it constantly, use it with faith, and thou shalt surely be a benefactor to thy brethren."

- Charles Spurgeon

"Prayer makes a godly man, and puts within him the mind of Christ, the mind of humility, of self-surrender, of service, of pity, and of prayer. If we really pray, we will become more like God, or else we will quit praying."

- E.M. Bounds

"Intercessory prayer is the purifying bath into which the individual and the community must enter every day."

- Dietrich Bonhoeffer

"God brings you to places, among people, and into certain conditions to accomplish a definite purpose through the intercession of the Spirit in you. Your part in intercessory prayer is not to agonize over how to intercede, but to use the everyday circumstances and people God puts around you by His providence to bring them before His throne, and to allow the Spirit in you the opportunity to intercede for them. In this way God is going to touch the whole world with His saints."

- Oswald Chambers

"The church that is not jealously protected by mighty intercession and sacrificial labors will before long become the abode of every evil bird and the hiding place for unsuspected corruption. The creeping wilderness will soon take over that church that trusts in its own strength and forgets to watch and pray."

- A. W. Tozer

"We may be forced to consume considerable time before the spirit cooperates. For example, God would like to enlarge the scope of our prayer to include the nations in order to defeat all the behind-the-scene works of Satan. Or He may want us to intercede for all sinners worldwide for the entire church."

- Watchman Nee

Please email prayer requests and praise reports to: akindewum@gmail.com

∽∾∾☉∾∽∾
REFERENCES
∽∾∾☉∾∽∾

Power BibleCD program © 2000 Phil Lindner, Online Publishing Inc., Michigan. (Version 2.5 – KJV). bible@mail.com

The Holy Bible (1611). *King James Version*. Trinitarian Bible Society, England (1991). (Cambridge University Press: Cambridge).

Internet Resources

https://books.google.com.ng/books?id=j0-tLkTKZBAC&pg=PA391&lpg=PA391&dq=william+barclay:+It+has+been+said+that+chastity+was+the+one+completely+new+virtue+which+Christianity+introduced+into+the+pagan+world&source=bl&ots

https://shepherdsofthelost.org

https://www.aglow.org

https://www.epm.org/resources/2009/Mar/28/great-quotes-prayer/

https://www.google.com/search?tbm=bks&q=inauthor:%22C.+Peter+Wagner%22&sa=X&ved=2ahUKEwiq1JaH2cbfAhXEx4MKHWCJDpQQ9AgwAHoECAoQAg

http://www.mountcalvarybaptist.org/site/user/files/1/ Week-2_Black_-Fredlyne_Self-Control.pdf

https://www.vocabulary.com

www.https//azquotes.com

www.ingramcontent.com/pod-product-compliance
Lightning Source LLC
Chambersburg PA
CBHW060803050426
42449CB00008B/1505